Bright As An Autumn Moon

MĀNOA 25:2

UNIVERSITY
OF HAWAI'I
PRESS

HONOLULU

Bright As An Autumn Moon

FIFTY POEMS FROM THE SANSKRIT

TRANSLATED BY

Andrew Schelling

FRANK STEWART

GENERAL EDITOR

Featuring Deccani miniature paintings from the late eighteenth century from an album (muraqqa') *compiled in the late nineteenth century, possibly later. The Walters Art Museum, Baltimore* [w.669].

Founded in 1988 by Robert Shapard and Frank Stewart

Mānoa is published twice a year. Subscriptions: U.S.A. and international—individuals $30 one year, $54 two years; institutions $50 one year, $90 two years; international airmail add $24 per year. Single copies: U.S.A. and international—individuals $20; institutions $30; international airmail add $12 per copy. Call toll free 1-888-UHPRESS. We accept checks, money orders, Visa, or MasterCard, payable to University of Hawai'i Press, 2840 Kolowalu Street, Honolulu, HI 96822, U.S.A. Claims for issues not received will be honored until 180 days past the date of publication; thereafter, the single-copy rate will be charged.

Mānoa gratefully acknowledges the support of the University of Hawai'i Administration and the University of Hawai'i College of Languages, Linguistics, and Literature; and additional support from the National Endowment for the Arts, the Hawai'i State Foundation on Culture and the Arts, and the Mānoa Foundation.

ART WORKS.
arts.gov

HAWAI'I
STATE FOUNDATION on CULTURE and the ARTS

the Mānoa Foundation

manoajournal.hawaii.edu
uhpress.hawaii.edu/journals/manoa
muse.jhu.edu (Project Muse)
jstor.org

Contents

Preface

The sixteen Deccani miniature paintings featured in this volume come from an album of ragmala—*visual representations of male and female musical modes or melodies. Now in a brown goatskin binding, the album, or codex, was formerly in an accordion format. The Walters Art Museum, Baltimore* [w.669].

India's Sanskrit poetry arose as a classical tradition in about the fourth century and continued into the twelfth, often subsidized at the courts of princes or warlords, or finding haven in huge Buddhist universities. Its main theme was erotic love. *Bright as an Autumn Moon* is a collection of poems from that full time span. Some have been recognized as superb Sanskrit lyrics for centuries, both within and outside India. Others are less celebrated perhaps, but each holds something to treasure. Every time I've translated one, and found what I thought a lovely match between languages, an impersonal thrill has raced through my blood. But there are not many people I can share that thrill with. Not at its deepest level, the level that goes back into the original language, takes stock of the words, the sounds, the cadences themselves, the simple astounding effect of these minute elements in combination.

The American scholars who write about Sanskrit poetry focus largely on cultural issues: linguistics, power dynamics, the role of women in Old India, erotic practices, history, caste, religion. These subjects—or rather these forces—ripple through every poem, sometimes close to the surface, sometimes hidden beneath. But poems also exceed these things. A poem carries more than its "meaning." This "more" includes musical values, images that raise bright scenes to our inner vision, ideas that occur inside the emotions. Because of this, poems slip free from explanation, and probably the fascination or bewilderment readers feel in their presence comes from how they illuminate cultural forces but always manage to escape paraphrase. This is what makes translation tricky. You cannot simply isolate a meaning, transfer it into another language, and pass it off as a good poem.

I believe every language has its own genius. Yes, there exist aspects of the poem that the translator wistfully has to leave behind in the original language, especially sound values. But every language you translate into will possess its own, equally subtle characteristics, some quality that a translator can find to devise an echo, a parallel effect. If I read Walter Benjamin correctly, he seems to say that translation is what makes a poem enter the deep stream of world consciousness.

There are mysteries of poetic craft. There is the magic of language (something to which Old India proved exceptionally alert). And there are poems where multiple ideas occur at the same time, even confounding or contradicting one another. Influenced by Tantric practices of coding language—to conceal meaning, to devise secrets for initiates, or to produce a subliminal or subconscious effect—the Sanskrit poets called these possibilities *sandhyā-bhāṣā,* or twilight speech. Modes of expression based on ambiguity, homology, dual meanings; linguistic events that get under your skin.

Linguist and South Asia scholar Murray B. Emeneau says,

> It is noteworthy and perhaps to be interpreted as a general tendency in Hindu culture to raise certain aspects of the subliminal to consciousness, that Hinduism in general and the Tantric sects in particular make extensive use in ritual and religious practice . . . of intrinsically meaningless vocables. For example, the famous *om* and *hum* and the not so famous *hrim, hrām, phat,* and many others.

This practice—using the power of seed sounds for psycho-spiritual effect—pervades poetry as well. The poets make use of two distinct levels at once: the meaning of the words, and the subliminal psychic discharge from "meaningless vocables" that underlie the words. Handbooks and *grimoires* of the period laid out for poets the way particular sounds evoke precise emotions.

The Sanskrit *kavi,* the poet, had a name for that which exceeds culture and politics and religion: *rasa. Rasa* is poetic power.

Anselm Hollo used to say translation is the closest reading you can give a poem. In his way of thinking, this book would then be a toolkit for close reading. Every year a group of dedicated students works on Sanskrit with me at Naropa University in Boulder, Colorado. I've compiled a casebook of poems to bring to class. On a surface level, I use these poems to illustrate how certain forms of grammar work, or how vocabulary or syntax contain a *śakti,* a singular power that animates the poem. Below the surface, I'm stirring the original poems to life. *Rasa* does not dwell in a poem on the page; nor is it tucked away in a realm of philosophy. *Rasa* emerges when the poem enters our bodies. How does this work? I have no ready answer. Abhinavagupta, Ānandavardhana, and other Indian writers have composed psycho-linguistic treatises that try to explain it.

So this collection, pulled from my workbooks, is meant to cast light on the poems in the original, before translation occurred, to reach back for something older, wilder, more primal, something the early poets discovered with pride and made into lyrics with the guidance of Sarasvatī, Indian goddess who presides over poetry and music. It is my hope that those who do not know the language will find in *Bright as an Autumn Moon* a way to gaze into the Sanskrit. And for those who know something of Sanskrit, a way to draw even closer. To stand eyebrow to eyebrow with the original poets.

For each verse, I have provided the *deva-nāgarī* original, plus a romanized version so readers can sound out the words if they don't know the North Indian writing system. I've also composed a list of equivalent meanings for each word and glossed the elegant compound words, hoping to show how they fit together. These lists are approximate, because words don't really have meanings. Words break into auras of meaning, clusters of meaning, shades, echoes, shadows of meaning. They carry other words inside themselves; they seep into each other. In a heavily inflected language like Sanskrit, it can be hard to define exactly what a word is. Thus I regard every so-called word as a metabolic creature. Set a number of them loose together, you get a small eco-zone. A zone lying far beyond the definitions a dictionary alone can give.

A little commentary sits beneath each of the poems. Ranging from a few sentences to a few pages, they describe where the poem is located in the tradition, tell something about the poet, or discuss how the writer used certain words or forms of grammar to achieve an effect. I may point out something about cadence, ambiguity, subversive vocabulary, sound values, or other aspects of craft. Here and there I've included cultural lore that may not be immediately obvious but gives dimension to the original.

If you want to read the translations by themselves and skip the rest of the material, I encourage it. You will taste the wild-game flavor of the Sanskrit tradition, bright beneath the hunter's moon. As a translator I'd hope for this. If you want to edge a bit closer, to stand for a moment between two languages and watch the moon as it rises, the rest of the material should help.

My thanks to the editors of the books and journals where some of these translations first appeared, for permission to reprint them.

I am deeply grateful to Rebecca Eland, who gave me courage to compile this book in the first place; her support and ongoing enthusiasm made it happen. My thanks to L. S. Summer for help with proofreading, and decisions about the original Sanskrit and thorny word lists. Then I want to remember my friend, fellow poet Anselm Hollo, for his dry, good-humored approach, and lifelong work at translation. Anselm died this year, leaving world poetry richer for having tracked through it. "Aren't we lucky," he once inscribed a book to me. "Let's remain so."

Note on Grammar and Spelling

Despite several thousand years of writing, Sanskrit remains an oral language, its vocal structure little changed. It makes widespread use of *sandhi* (joining), a kind of ecology of sound. When two words come up against one another, the abutting sounds can change to help one's mouth pass from word to word. Sanskrit's standard written script, *deva-nāgarī,* changes its letters to reflect the changes in pronunciation. (Most languages contain ecological sound changes, but in English we don't alter our spellings in order to codify them. Notice, for example, the difference in how one pronounces *the: the child* versus *the infant.*) In the vocabulary list accompanying each poem, I've generally returned words to what they look like before *sandhi* occurs. This makes them easier to look up in a dictionary.

There's an internal *sandhi* too—changes that occur inside words. Any good Sanskrit grammar gives the details. If you are interested in the sounds of the language as spoken, the grammar books can match written characters to sounds. Keep in mind that long vowels and diphthongs are held longer than short vowels. Sanskrit poetic meters are mostly quantitative, built on sequences of short and long (light and heavy) syllables. Stress on syllables is secondary.

Sanskrit writing and typesetting can be a bit inconsisent. Some poems show up in two or more collections with slight shifts in vocabulary or spelling. I have given the poems as my source texts do, using the *deva-nāgarī* as they use it. Where something odd appears, it is because I want to honor the poems as they came to me, not second-guess the old masters.

One other characteristic worth noting is Sanskrit's use of compound words: two or more words put together. These can be quite long, joining many nouns, adjectives, and verbal elements. In this way the speakers accomplish what other languages may have to do with lots of clauses, or multiple sentences. Compounds look forbidding at first, but they make the poetry swift, light-footed, compressed. Few words, much information.

A *bahuvṛhi* is a compound used as an adjective. It often takes the place of the person or object described. Epithets, for example, tend to be *bahuvṛhis:* "wheel turner" for a powerful warlord (he sets the universe in motion); holder of the "horned bow" for a constellation identified with Vishnu. Poets make these up to suit their needs. In the opening poem of *Bright as an Autumn Moon, śarad-indu-sundara-rucih̤* is such a compound: autumn-moon-beauty-shine. These four words, lined up in a particular order, are an adjective for *girāṃ devī,* goddess of speech. In English you would say something like "goddess who is bright with the splendor of an autumn moon."

List of Abbreviations

Grammatical Terms

abs. absolute
adj. adjective
adv. adverb
bv. cmpd. *bahuvṛhi* compound (noun or adjective)
emph. emphatic
excl. exclamation
f. feminine
imp. imperative
ind. indeclinable (generally an adverb)
inst. instrumental
loc. locative
m. masculine
poss. possessive (genitive)
voc. vocative

Source Texts

AD Western recension (Arjunavarmadeva, Devadhar)
AM Amaruśataka
AS Abhijñāna-Śakuntalā
GG Gīta-Govinda
HG Hemacandra's Grammar
KS Kumārasambhava
MD Meghadūta
PE The Peacock's Egg
PRM A Poem at the Right Moment
SP Sanskrit Poetesses
SR Subhāṣitaratnakoṣa

शरदिन्दुसुन्दररुचिश्चेतसि सा मे गिरां देवी ।
अपहृत्य तमः संततमर्थानखिलान् प्रकाशयतु ।।

śaradindusundararuciś cetasi sā me girāṃ devī
apahṛtya tamaḥ saṃtatam arthān akhilān prakāśayatu

śarad. autumn
indu. moon
sundara. beauty
ruciḥ. splendor, brightness
cetasi. on the heart
sā. she
me. my, of me
girāṃ. of language
devī. goddess
apahṛtya. having removed
tamaḥ. darkness
saṃtatam. covering, extending, all-encompassing
arthān. things, elements
akhilān. without gap, nothing left out, all
prakāśayatu. let (her) illuminate or reveal

Shining with the Luster

Shining with the luster
of moon in autumn
may She, Goddess Language,
stripping from my
heart the endless woven darkness,
cast the nature of all
things into light.

Viśvanātha opens his fourteeth-century *Sahitya Darpaṇa* (Mirror of Composition) with this invocation. His book is a volume of poetics, demonstrating how poetry works. In classical India, where all crafts or arts fulfilled a spiritual purpose, this meant it was also a book of yoga wisdom, liberation being the goal. Hence his *Mirror* is viewed as a poetry-spirit handbook. Viśvanātha invites the blessing of the deity who guides his writing. To open one's book with a *stuti* (praise poem) would be traditional and necessary for success. Benedictions remove obstacles to important work. Gir Devī, or Goddess Language, is Sarasvatī, who cares for three interrelated arts—poetry, music, and scholarship. She rides a swan—its beating wings the principles of breath and rhythm—and in her hands she holds a book and a *vīṇā*, a stringed musical instrument.

Old India, civilized as she is, stands far closer to the archaic than to our contemporary post-postmodern world. Archaic cultures hold deep-rooted beliefs in the power of language. Prayer, invocation, mantra, benediction, vow, curse, love charm—these are not merely expressive statements or poetic flourishes. They are language-magic tools; poets consider them effective, even irreversible. In our current world, language is regarded as contested territory, something that can fetter human freedom—"the prison house of language." Viśvanātha sees human utterance the way poets do: a field of liberation. The goddess who animates it can strip from one's heart the *tamas* (darkness) that is *saṃtatam* (all-covering, woven, spread over). At the same time, Viśvanātha asks her to illuminate all things *(artha)*. *Artha* can also be defined as "meaning," as in the meaning of a word or poem. *Reveal things and their meanings,* he asks: things in their original nature.

FROM THE SUBHĀṢITARATNAKOṢA

Anonymous

कृत्वा नूपुरमूकता चरणयाः सयम्य नावामणान्
    उद्दामध्वनिपिण्डितान् परिजने किंचिन्न निद्रायिते ।
कस्मै कुप्यसि यावदस्मि चलितातावद्विधिप्रेरितः
    काश्मीरीकुचकुम्भसंभ्रमहरः शीतांशुरभ्युद्यतः ॥

[SR 834]

kṛtvā nūpuramūkatāṃ caraṇayoḥ saṃyamya nīvīmaṇīn
    uddāmadhvanipiṇḍitān parijane kiṃcinna nidrāyite
kasmai kupyasi yāvad asmi calitā tāvad vidhi preritaḥ
    kāśmīrīkucakumbhasaṃbhramaharaḥ śītāṃśurabhy udyataḥ

kṛtvā. having made
nūpura. anklets
mūkatāṃ. silent
caraṇayoḥ. on my feet
saṃyamya. having bound
nīvī. sash, cloth waistband
maṇīn. jewels
uddāma. unrestrained, noisy
dhvani. noise, roar
piṇḍitān. cluster
parijane. company of people
kiṃcinna. somehow
nidrāyite. made (or watched) them go to sleep
kasmai. why
kupyasi. are you angry
yāvat [and] *tāvat.* right then, just when
asmi. I was
calitā. set forth
vidhi. (voc.) O Fate
preritaḥ. you drove, impelled
kāśmīrī. (like a) Kashmiri girl's (this and the following words through *haraḥ* are a bv. cmpd. with moon)
kuca-kumbha. breast
saṃbhrama-haraḥ. over my path (literally, obstructing my path)
śītāṃśurabhi. white, cold moon
udyataḥ. up-risen

Having Silenced the Silver

Having silenced the silver
chains at my ankles,
bound up the noisy
jewels on my waistband,
and watched the nearby
households go to sleep—
Fate, why are you angry?
I'd just set forth
when you spurred the cold
new-risen moon, bright
as a Kashmiri girl's breast,
over the open road.

The speaker sets out for a perilous night meeting with her lover, a theme depicted in countless Indian miniature paintings. The anonymous poet uses sharp syllables driven by *ū* and *ī*, which sound like the clinking of jewelry: *nūpura-mūkatām* and *nīvī-maṇīn*. They highlight the contrast between the care the young woman takes to muffle her bright ornaments, and the vulnerability of her moonlit form. Seeing the cold bright moon as a pale girl's breast excites in the poem both desire and the woman's heightened fear, lest she be discovered.

This poem is from one of the significant Sanskrit anthologies, the *Subhāṣitaratnakoṣa* (Anthology of Poetry Gems), a collection of 1,738 lyrics distributed through fifty thematic chapters. The editor, Vidyākara, was a twelfth-century Buddhist abbot of Jagaddala monastery, in Bengal. A man of wide and varied tastes, he showed no qualms about including openly erotic poems in his collection. Flanked by chapters on the seasons, on Buddha, on various Indic deities, and on wealth, poverty, fame, and so forth, the core chapters focus on the phases or seasons of erotic love.

Vidyākara's anthology was entirely lost until this century, when two explorers, a few years apart, happened upon a readable twelfth-century palm-leaf manuscript, probably Vidyākara's personal copy. They each found it in a barn at the Ngor monastery in Tibet, about a day's journey by foot from Shigatse. Jagaddala monastery was destroyed during Muslim incursions around 1207 CE. Its last abbot, Śakśrībhadra, may have fled to Tibet in 1204. He would have carried books, mementos from former abbots, images, and other monastic treasures for preservation. Most likely he took with him Vidyākara's manuscript.

The manuscript resurfaced first in 1934, happened on by Rahula Sankrityayana, an Indian pandit and good scholar of Sanskrit who was possibly traveling through Tibet as a British spy. A few years later Giuseppe Tucci, the noted Italian art collector and scholar of Buddhism, came across the same manuscript. Each managed to produce, under challenging conditions, photographic plates of very poor quality ("execrable," says one account), and to transport them out of Tibet.

The palm-leaf manuscript has not been seen again. It held about a thousand poems. A copy of the same anthology, this one produced on paper and housed in Kathmandu, holds 1,728 poems, leading Daniel H. H. Ingalls (who translated the entire collection) to speculate that Vidyākara worked on the manuscript for years. The copy in the monastery at Ngor would have been an early version, a work in progress.

The way Vidyākara's book surfaced eighty years ago after nearly a thousand years, but has not been seen since, seems a fitting emblem of the tattered, fragmentary nature of Sanskrit poetry.

FROM THE AMARUŚATAKA

संदष्टाधरपल्लवा सचकितं हस्ताग्रमाधुन्वती
मा मा मुञ्च शठेति कोपवचनैरानर्तितभ्रूलता ।
सीत्काराञ्चितलोचना सपूलकं यैश्चुम्बिता मानिनी
प्राप्तं तैरमृतं श्रमाय मथितो मूढैः सुरैः सागरः ।।
[AM 4]

saṃdaṣṭādharapallavā sacakitaṃ hastāgramādhunvatī
mā mā muñca śaṭheti kopavacanair ānartitabhrūlatā
sītkārāñcitalocanā sapūlakaṃ yaiś cumbitā māninī
prāptaṃ tair amṛtaṃ śramāya mathito mūḍhaiḥ suraiḥ sāgaraḥ

saṃdaṣṭa. nipped, bitten
adhara. lip
pallavā. bud, sprout
sacakitaṃ. (adv.) timidly, with alarm
hasta-agrama-adhunvatī. (bv. cmpd.) she who is "hand-tip-shaking"
mā mā. don't don't!
muñca. (imp.) leave
śaṭha. (voc.) O cheater, rogue
iti. [quotation marks]
kopa-vacanair. with angry words
ānartita-bhrūlatā. (bv. cmpd.) with dancing vine-like brow
sītkāra-āñcita-locanā. (bv. cmpd.) with oblique eyes
sapulakaṃ. bristling with desire, thrilling
yaiḥ. by those who
cumbitā. kissed
māninī. prideful woman
prāptaṃ. obtained
taiḥ. by them
amṛtaṃ. juice of immortality
śramāya. with toil, labor
mathito. (adj. with ocean) churned
mūḍhaiḥ. (adj. with gods) foolish
suraiḥ. by the gods
sāgaraḥ. ocean

Tender Lip Bitten

Tender lip bitten she
shakes her fingers alarmed—
hisses a fierce
Don't you dare and her
eyebrows leap like a vine.
Who steals a kiss from a
proud woman flashing her eyes
secures *amṛta*.
The gods—fools—
churned the ocean for
nothing.

After enormous labor, the gods collectively managed to raise *amṛta*, the drink of immortality (Greek, *ambrosia*), from the ocean floor. They concealed it on the far side of the moon, away from the grasp of dark forces who would steal and drink it in order to become dreadfully powerful. A life-bestowing fluid stored on the moon, *amṛta* became identified with *soma*, potent vision-inducing drink of the Vedas. As precious generative fluids, both *amṛta* and *soma* have strong sexual implications—they are the juices of life.

The *Amaruśataka* (Hundred Poems of Amaru) opens in traditional fashion with verses that invoke two ardent deities, the Great Goddess and Śiva. Then comes a twist: two verses—this the second—that mock and dismiss the gods. Even the gods—the poet observes are disarmed by desire. Let the gods toil away, churning *amṛta* from the ocean depths. Love is the real beverage that overcomes death.

FROM THE AMARUŚATAKA

रात्रौ वारिभरालसाम्बुदरवोद्विग्नेना जाताश्रुणा
पान्थेनात्मवियोगदुःखपिशुनं गीतं तथोत्कण्ठया ।
आस्तां जीवितहारिणः प्रवसनालापस्य संकीर्तनं
मानस्यापि जलाञ्जलिः सरभसं लोकेन दत्तो यथा ॥
[AM 46]

rātrau vāribharālasāmbudaravodgvignenā jātāśruṇā
pānthenātmaviyogaduḥkhapiśunaṃ gītaṃ tathotkaṇṭhayā
āstāṃ jīvitahāriṇaḥ pravasanālāpasya saṃkīrtanaṃ
mānasyāpi jalāñjaliḥ sarabhasaṃ lokena datto yathā

rātrau. in the night
vāri-bhara-ālasa-ambuda-rava-udvignena. (bv. cmpd.) by him (the traveler) stricken by thunder from the cloud, slow and weighted with rain
jātāśruṇā. (bv. cmpd.) he with rising tears
pānthena. traveler
ātma-viyoga. own separation
duḥkha. grief
piśunaṃ. (adj. with song) telling, disclosing
gītaṃ. song
tathā. in this way
utkaṇṭhayā. grieving (literally, lifting the throat)
āstāṃ. must be (with traveling)
jīvita-hāriṇaḥ. life destroying
pravasana. living far-off, traveling
ālāpasya. talk
samkīrtanaṃ. praise, glory, boasting
mānasya. pride
api. then
jalāñjaliḥ. water or funerary offering (here: respect, observance; metaphorically, silence)
sarabhasaṃ. quickly
lokena. by the people
datto. (is) given
yathā. thus

Night
turbulent overhead clouds
and a ripple of thunder.
The traveler
stung with tears
sings of a faraway girl.
Oh traveling
is a kind of death,
the village people hear it,
lower their heads
and suddenly quit their
proud tales
of adventure.

You could gather hundreds of Indian poems, sculptures, murals, and paintings that depict a person singing or playing music: love songs, work songs, ballads, folk lyrics—all carrying a subtle message for the listener or viewer. In particular the poets were sensitive to songs of heartbreak or separation from a beloved. Picture the villagers—many of them having returned home just ahead of the monsoons—seated by an evening fire, outdoing one another with accounts of their adventures in faraway places, when a song of grief cuts the night.

Travel in Old India was a necessity, but with the onset of the monsoon season, traders, merchants, soldiers, and pilgrims returned home to wait out the rainy months. This is the time in India when rain swells the rivers, roads get washed out, and travel becomes arduous or perilous. But monsoon season is also when Earth puts forth sweet blossoms, fresh grass emerges, and animal and bird life seems to waken. The poets regarded it as the time when, after long journeys home, humans make love to the sound of rainfall in the refreshing nights. To be caught on the road when the rains begin is the gravest misfortune. The villagers—hearing the traveler sing—give up glorifying travel, which steals one's life, and make a funerary offering (*jalāñjali*) to their own boastful stories.

Here, the anonymous poet pays quiet tribute to the origins of poetry which lie in folksong. India has a long-held belief that village life and its repertoire of songs provide the best source for poetry. In their earliest verse collections, urban or courtly cultures cast a wistful, admiring look at the lives of rural or hunting people. Ethnopoetics. You find this tribute to origins in China's *Book of Songs*, Japan's *Manyōshū*, and in *The Greek*

Anthology; Shakespeare; Coleridge and Wordsworth in *Lyrical Ballads;* Blake's *Songs of Innocence and Experience;* García Lorca's *Gypsy Ballads;* and Lorine Niedecker's *New Goose.* Each poet wrote from his or her own folk tradition.

I wonder if the speaker in this poem isn't a traveler, himself caught on the road as the clouds thicken.

गाढालिङ्गनवामनीकृतकुचप्रोद्भिन्नरोमोद्गमा
सान्द्रस्नेहरसातिरेकविगलत्काञ्चीप्रदेशाम्बरा ।
मा मा मानद माति मामलमिति क्षामाक्षरोल्लापिनी
सुप्ता किं नु मृता नु किं मनसि मे लीना विलीना नु किम् ॥
[AM 35]

gāḍhāliṅganavāmanīkṛtakucaprodbhinnaromodgamā
sāndrasneharasātir ekavigalat kāñcīpradeśāmbarā
mā mā mānada māti māmalam iti kṣāmākṣarollāpinī
suptā kiṃ nu mṛtā nu kiṃ manasi me līnā vilīnā nu kim

gāḍhāliṅgana-vāmanī-kṛta-kuca-prodbhinna-romodgamā. (bv. cmpd.)
gāḍhāliṅgana. tight embrace
vāmanī-kṛta. flattened, pressed down
kuca. breasts
prodbhinna. burst forth
roma-udgamā. pubic area
sāndra. smooth, soft
sneharasātiḥ. (bv. cmpd.) affection, filled with love or desire
eka-vigalat. at once coming untied
kañcī. girdle or undergarment
pradeśa. zone, area
ambarā. clothes
mā mā. don't don't!
mānada. (voc.) O ravager (literally, destroyer of respect)
māti. don't, enough
māmalam. enough for me!
iti. [quotation marks]
kṣāma-akṣara-ullāpinī. (bv. cmpd.) (f.) weak-word-speaker
suptā. sleep (did she sleep)
kiṃ nu. what was it, how is it
mṛtā. dead (is she dead, did she die)
nu kiṃ. what, how is it
manasi. in (my) heart
me. my, mine
līnā. pressed into
vilīnā. dissolved, absorbed
nu kiṃ. or was she

Her Breasts

Her breasts
flattened against me
her flesh seemed to ripple
at her thighs the thin
silk parted.
I heard a mute *Don't—*
don't—this is enough for me—
did she sleep, did she die then?
sink in my heart
completely dissolve?

In the Sanskrit, the first two lines of this poem are comprised of three *bahuvṛhi* compounds describing the woman and her garments. The third line captures the woman's exclamations with a nearly animal bleat: *mā mā mānada māti.* The questions that follow her cry recall Yeats's words in "Crazy Jane Looks at the Dancers":

> Did he die or did she die?
> Seemed to die or died they both?

Sound out the final line of the original Sanskrit poem here. You'll find a repetition, as insistent and fierce as Yeats's, that drives this poem to its close. Another poem from the *Amaruśataka,* "She's in My House," carries the repetition of a single long syllable even further.

रोहन्तौ प्रथमं ममोरसि तव प्राप्तौ विवृद्धिं स्तनौ
    संल्लापास्तव वाक्यभंगिमिलनान्मोग्ध्यं परं त्याजिताः ।
घात्रीकण्ठमपास्य बाहुलतिके कण्ठे तवासञ्जिते
    निर्दाक्षिण्य करोमि किन्नु विशिखाप्येषा न पन्थास्तव ॥

[AM 87]

rohantau prathamaṃ mamorasi tava prāptau vivṛddhiṃ stanau
    saṃllāpās tava vākyabhaṃgimilanānmogdhyaṃ paraṃ tyājitāḥ
ghātrīkaṇṭham apāsya bāhulatike kaṇṭhe tavāsañjite
    nirdākṣiṇya karomi kinnu viśikhāpy eṣā na panthās tava

rohantau. budding
prathamaṃ. at first
mamorasi. on (your) chest
tava. your
prāptau. against
vivṛddhiṃ. growing up
stanau. breasts
saṃllāpās. conversation
tava. with you
vākya. speech
bhaṃgi. mode, manner
milanān. coming together
mogdhyaṃ. innocence, simplicity
paraṃ. next
tyājitāḥ. abandoned
ghātrī. nursemaid's
kaṇṭham. neck
apāsya. having released
bāhulatike. (these) arms (also creepers)
kaṇṭhe. on (your) neck
tava. your
āsañjite. clung
nirdākṣiṇya. deceiver, devious one
karomi kinnu. I can do what?
viśikhā. road, neighborhood
api-eṣā. this
na. is not
panthās tava. your path

My Breasts at First

My breasts at first
little buds
grew plump under your hands.
My speech
instructed by yours
lost its native simplicity.
What shall I do?
These arms
left my old nursemaid's neck
to creep around yours,
but you no longer
    set foot in the neighborhood.

For centuries the *Amaruśataka* (Hundred Poems of Amaru, ca. ninth century) has been attributed to a poet named Amaru. However, seventy of the poems appear in Vidyākara's *Subhāṣitaratnakoṣa* (see page 5), most of them credited to other poets. Vidyākara compiled his anthology in the eleventh century, so it seems likely the *Amaruśataka* is also an early anthology. Western scholars have tended to regard it as a collection, but many people in India know it as a single poem-cycle composed by one author.

The legend that accompanies the poems in the *Amaruśataka* gives them curious metaphysical weight. The renowned religious reformer Shankara (ca. eighth century)—whose philosophical writings loom as large as anyone's in India—was engaging an opponent in public debate. He was roundly beating his rival when his opponent's wife stepped in. She silenced Shankara with a series of clever metaphysical questions couched in the language of sexual love. Shankara, celibate and inexperienced in the art of love, could not answer. He asked for a hundred nights to prepare a response. Leaving the stage, he gathered some close students and entrusted them with his body while, through powers of yoga, he projected his spirit-self into the body of Amaru, a recently deceased king of Kashmir. The corpse, lying on the pyre awaiting cremation, wakened to life.

For a hundred nights, Shankara studied love with Amaru's harem girls. During this time, he memorialized his experiences in lyrics—one for each night of bittersweet pleasure. After the hundredth night had lapsed—and he'd thrown in a few more for luck—Shankara returned to his own body. I suppose he left Amaru's corpse to its fate.

Reentering the hall of debate, he vanquished his female opponent. He later committed to writing the poems that had sealed his victory, signing them with Amaru's name.

While the Amaru collection has poems of romantic tenderness, humor, tangy eroticism, and playful lovemaking, more poems treat the other side: separation, anguished longing, jealousy, betrayal, searing heartache, and the like.

नान्तःप्रवेशमरुणद्विमुखी न चासी-
दाचष्ट रोषपरुषाणि न चाक्षराणि ।
सा केवलं सरलपक्ष्मभिरक्षिपातैः
कान्तं विलोकितवती जननिर्विशेषम् ॥
[AM 99]

nāntaḥpraveśam aruṇad vimukhī na cāsīd
ācaṣṭa roṣaparuṣāṇi na cākṣarāṇi
sā kevalaṃ saralapakṣmabhir akṣipātaiḥ
kāntaṃ vilokitavatī jananirviśeṣam

na. not
antaḥpraveśam. entry
aruṇat. she blocked
vimukhī. (adj.) face averted
na. not
ca. and, either
asīt. was
ācaṣṭa. spoken
roṣa. angry
paruṣāṇi. harsh, severe
na ca. nor
akṣarāṇi. words, sounds
sā. she
kevalaṃ. only
sarala. artless, straight ahead
pakṣmabhir. through (her) eyelashes
akṣi-pātaiḥ. with a gaze, with glances
kāntaṃ. (her) lover
vilokitavatī. (a *ktavatu,* a verb turned into an adj.) she looked at, regarded
jana. (as a) person, man
nirviśeṣam. not different; ordinary

She Did Nothing to Bar the Door

She did nothing to
bar the door
did not turn her face away
there were no brittle words.
She just gazed with indifferent eyes through
steady lashes.
He could have been anyone.

An example of Sanskrit's lapidary style; a more talkative tradition would construct a novella around this scene. The old poets valued restraint, understatement, or suggestion: emotion conveyed through few words. Here the feeling is vivid even if we know none of the dramatic details. Certain Sanskrit poems—not dressed up; free of adornment—were prized for using no figures of speech. Avoidance of ornament, though, was itself considered a poetic figure, an *alaṃkāra*.

प्रसादे सा दिशि दिशि च सा पृष्टतः सा पुरः सा
    पर्यंके सा पथि पथि च सा तद्वियोगातुरस्य ।
हंहो चेतः प्रकृतिरपरा नास्ति मे कापि सा सा
    सा सा सा सा जगति सकले कोऽयमद्वैतवादः ॥

[AD p121]

prasāde sā diśi diśi ca sā pṛṣṭataḥ sā puraḥ sā
    paryaṅke sā pathi pathi ca sā tadviyogāturasya
haṃho cetaḥ prakṛtir aparā nāsti me kāpi sā sā
    sā sā sā sā jagati sakale ko'yam advaitavādaḥ

prasāde. in front (or, in the house)
sā. she (is)
diśi diśi. direction direction (in every)
ca. and
sā. she
pṛṣṭataḥ. behind (west)
sā. she
puraḥ. in front (east)
sā. she
paryaṃke. on (my) bed, couch
sā. she
pathi pathi. path (after) path
ca. and
sā. she
tad-viyoga-āturasya. (bv. cmpd. with *me*) of this feverish separation from her
tat. (pronoun) from her
viyoga. separation
āturasya. *(ātura)* sickness, disease
haṃho. (excl.) oh, ah
cetaḥ. heart
prakṛtir. Nature, primal matter
aparā. apart from
na asti. there is no
me. for or of me
kā-api. some woman
sā sā sā sā sā sā. she she she she she she
jagati. in the universe
sakale. entire, whole
ko'yam. so what (is this)
advaita-vādaḥ. creed *(vāda)* of the Non-dualists

She's in My House

She's in my house
she's west and east
she trails behind me she goes
out ahead
she's in my bed on path
after path
what a fever—I can't
even see Nature now that she's left me—
just she she she she she she
across the whole wheeling planet.
And Non-dualism
they say is for yogins.

The *Amaruśataka* shows up in at least four versions, differing in what poems they present and in what order. Each version is associated with a region or direction in India. This poem only appears in a Western manuscript. If the entire Amaru collection were not comprised of erotic or love poetry, one could read this as a devotional poem to the Great Goddess. Its language plays off philosophical and religious terms. *Prakṛtī* (Nature) refers to primal matter or the feminine principle; *a-dvaita* is a principal school of belief, Non-dualism. Even the complaint at the woman's (or Goddess's) distance and the devotee's obsessive illness, *ātura*, is completely in line with Śakta or Kālī worship. The poetry of Rāmprasād Sen and Kamalakanta Bhattacharya in Bengal of the eighteenth and nineteenth centuries rests on a similar edge between praise and complaint, sometimes called *nindā-stuti*, praise in the form of abusive reproach.

The cry *sā sā sā sā sā sā* is unlike anything else I've seen in Sanskrit poetry. Repetition, however, is a standard practice in religious verse, as it is in song traditions. Repetition taken to non-sensical lengths is common to mystical and tantric texts, mantra and *dharaṇi.* I cannot tell if the poet is being ironic, or feeling devastated, devout, mocking, heartbroken, or is speaking from some extreme state in which all these emotions meet.

मञ्चे रोमाञ्चितान्.गी राति-मृदित-तनोः कर्कटी-वाटिकायां
कान्तस्यान्.गे प्रमोदादुभय-भुज-परिश्ष्वक्त-कण्ठे निलीना ।
पादेन प्रेन्.खयन्ती मुखरयति मुहुः पामरी फेरवाणां
रात्रावुत्रास-हेतोर्वृति-शिखर-लता-लम्बिनीं कम्बु-मालाम् ॥

[SP 108]

mañce romāñcitāṅgī ratimṛditatanoḥ karkaṭīvāṭikāyāṃ
kāntasyāṅge pramodād ubhayabhujapariṣvakta kaṇṭhe nilīnā
pādena preṅkhayantī mukharayati muhuḥ pāmarī pheravāṇāṃ
rātrāvutrāsahetor vṛtiśikharalatālambinīṃ kambumālām

mañce. (loc.) on a platform couch or bed
romāñcitāṅgī. (bv.cmp.) with hair bristling on (her) limbs
ratimṛditatanoḥ. (bv. cmpd.) the youth exhausted with lovemaking
karkaṭī. cucumber
vāṭikāyāṃ. in the garden
kāntasyāṅge. (bv. cmpd.) to (her) lover's body
pramodād. from pleasure
ubhaya. both
bhuja. desire
pariṣvakta. embraced, encircled
kaṇṭhe. around his neck
nilīnā. clinging to, enwrapping
pādena. with a foot
preṅkhayantī. rattling, jostling
mukharayati. (she) jangles
muhuḥ. now and again, repeatedly
pāmarī. tribal girl
pheravāṇāṃ. of jackals
rātrau. in the night
trāsa. fear, fright
hetoḥ. for the purpose
vṛtiśikharalatālambinīṃ. (bv. cmpd. with necklace) fence-post-vine-hanging
kambu. shell
mālām. necklace

On Makeshift Bedding

On makeshift
bedding in the cucumber
garden,
the hill-tribe girl
clings to her
exhausted lover.
Limbs still chafing
with pleasure, dissolving
against him she
now and again with
one bare foot
jostles a shell necklace
that hangs from a
vine on the fence—
rattling it
through the night,
scaring the jackals off.

Vidyā is the earliest known and in many ways the preeminent woman poet of Sanskrit. A Western scholar once called her "the Sappho of India." Her poem unfolds in a precise succession of images: the bed (a *mañca* is a raised platform in a field where a watchman is stationed to keep cattle or birds from damaging the crops), then the girl's bristling skin, her lover, the cucumber garden. Then her foot, night, invisible jackals, and the rattling shell necklace. How strange the jackals seem. I know of no comparable poem in the Sanskrit tradition.

The word here for jackal is not the common *sṛgāla* (source of our English word *jackal*) but a mimic word that approximates their sound: *phe-rava* (howl-crier). The golden jackal (*Canis aureus*) is widespread in India. It inhabits an ecological niche similar to that of the North American coyote, moving mostly at night, around the edges of villages, through the fields—a creature of inbetween spaces, a marauder, a thief. The lovers are vivid, lit by the poem's images. Everything is dark—in the fields far from the village—and full of menace. How precious, how fragile, the meeting of lovers. Vidyā seems to say we have only the passion of our relationships—a vulnerable sphere of closeness and comfort. Otherwise, "the darkness surrounds us" with its unseen peril.

VIDYĀ

मलिनहुतभुगधूमश्यामैर्दिशो मलिना धनै-
रविरलतृणैः श्यामा भूमिर्नवोद्गतकन्दलैः ।
सुरतसुभगो नूनं कालः स एव समागतो
मरणशरणा यस्मिन्नेते भवन्ति वियोगिनः ॥

[SP 127]

malinahutabhugadhūmaśyāmair diśo malinā dhanair
aviralatṛṇaiḥ śyāmā bhūmir navodgatakandalaiḥ
suratasubhago nūnaṃ kālaḥ sa eva samāgato
maraṇaśaraṇā yasminn ete bhavanti viyoginaḥ

malina. dark colored, black, dark gray, mendicant
huta-bhuga. "oblation eater," fire, fire-sacrifice, Vedic offering
dhūma. smoke, vapor, incense
śyāmaiḥ. with darkness
diśo. the directions or quarters of the sky
malinā. darkness
dhanaiḥ. (adj. with grass) plenty, abundant
avirala. dense, close, tangled
tṛnaiḥ. grass
śyāmā. dark
bhūmiḥ. earth
nava-udgata. newly arisen
kandalaiḥ. a white-flowering plant which appears plentifully and all at once with the rains
surata. lovemaking
subhago. eating (or lovemaking)
nūnaṃ. now
kālaḥ. time
sa. it
eva. surely
samāgato. to come together, draw close, make love
maraṇa-śaraṇā. (bv. cmpd.) they who go to death for refuge
yasmin. from those (who are beloved)
ete. these
bhavanti. they are, become
viyoginaḥ. those separated (from their lovers)

Dark Clouds

Dark clouds
mount the directions,
the sky
seems tossed
with flame and vapor.
Dark earth
presses white blossoms
out of the tangled grass.
Time now
to draw close,
talk, eat, make love.
Whoever's lover
has left her
goes to the pavilion
of Death.

Over the poem, over the poet's mood, clouds appear, pregnant with rain. This seasonal imagery—the slow building of monsoon clouds—is shorthand for the arousal of sexual moods. Do I detect in the repeated accumulation of rainclouds in Sanskrit poetry a whiff of shamanism, sympathetic magic, or animist weather control? By arousing erotic moods, can humans draw rain to the landscapes of India, which by late winter become parched?

Vidyā came from a highly refined world, more civilized and monumental—as well as far more ancient—than Homer's. The gods in her India seem shadowy, a bit like the Greek pantheon did for Shakespeare, Shelley, or Keats. Whoever they may be, by Vidyā's day the old Vedic *devas* that govern the elements (fire, wind, thunderbolt) have withdrawn into the distance. Of them, only whispers or echoes remain. Certainly they take no active role—are not meddlers—in human affairs. Nor do they hold much power. They cannot ward off death. Only love has that capability. When love departs, life goes also—to the mansion or sanctuary of the king of the underworld. The membrane separating the two realms, this and the other world, is perilously thin—a terrible truth that runs through so much early poetry. I'm reminded of Japanese poet Issa: "We pick flowers / on the roof / of hell" (translated by Robert Hass).

Vidyā complicates the beauty and gloom of her poem by conjuring the ecology in terms that sound liturgical. The dark sky is *malina*, a religious mendicant, the flaming horizon *huta-bhuga*, a Vedic fire sacrifice, the clouds *dhūma*, incense. Religion, love, and death converge in the poem. The formula *maraṇa-śaraṇā* (death-refuge or sanctuary-of-death) is a twist on religious themes.

This use of double meanings has been called *sandhyā-bhāṣā* (twilight speech). As with puns, two or more meanings land on a single word. In some cases it requires a string of words or phrases to generate the twilight, the shadow meanings, the echo of other texts, or to conceal one poem under another. In this verse, Vidyā has constructed a language-within-language that speaks on several psychic levels at once.

In the years before World War II, the French poet René Daumal devised a method of "vertical" translation to get at such layered meanings in Sanskrit. His translations look like worksheets, columns of possible words all reaching your eye simultaneously. "The words placed beneath a word of the text denote principal images or thoughts evoked by the word . . . by associations of meaning, sound, or etymology," he explains. "Words in parentheses denote a literal or strictly etymological translation . . . the words in brackets are not in the text but are implied." As he recognizes, a translation can pack in levels of meaning, but other powers of poetry are lost: the singular weave of rhythm, bright image, and sound.

VIDYĀ

प्रियसखि विपद्दण्डप्रान्तप्रपातपरंपरा-
    परिचयचले चिन्ताचक्रे निधाय विधिः खलः ।
मृदमिव बलात्पिण्डीकृत्य प्रगल्भकुलालवद्
    भ्रमयति मनो नो जानीमः किमत्र विधास्यति ॥

[SR 1267]

priyasakhi vipaddaṇḍaprāntaprapātaparaṃparā-
    paricayacale cintācakre nidhāya vidhiḥ khalaḥ
mṛdam iva balāt piṇḍīkṛtya pragalbhakulālavad
    bhramayati mano no jānīmaḥ kim atra vidhāsyati

priya. dear
sakhi. friend
vipaddaṇḍaprāntaprapātaparaṃparā-paricayacale. (bv. cmpd. with wheel) literally, which turns by its contact with a series of strokes from the staff-tip of misfortune
vipad. adversity, misfortune, calamity
daṇḍa. (m.) stick, handle, staff, rod, scepter; also sovereignty, power, authority
prānta. point, tip
prapāta. movements, startings
paraṃparā. series, succession
pari-caya. heaping up, contact
cale. moving, turning, loosing
cintā. anxiety
cakre. on a wheel
nidhāya. having placed
vidhiḥ. law, rule, fate (here personified)
khalaḥ. lowly, mischievous, cruel
mṛdam. earth, clay
iva. like, as
balāt. with force, forcibly
piṇḍī. lump, ball
kṛtya. having done, made
pragalbha. resolute
kulāla. (m.) potter
vat. like
bhramayati. (causative) he moves, sets in motion
mano. (my) heart
no. not
jānīmaḥ. we (I) know
kim. what
atra. here
vidhāsyati. he will form, make, build

Fate

Fate is a cruel
and proficient potter,
my friend. Forcibly
spinning the wheel
of anxiety, he lifts misfortune
like a cutting tool. Now
having kneaded my heart
like a lump of clay,
he lays it on his
wheel and gives a spin.
What he intends to produce
I cannot tell.

Why is it that the potter's wheel, the cartwheel, the wheeling stars, or the roulette wheel remain the most potent symbols of chance or fate? Vidyā takes the image a step further by naming adversity or calamity the shaping force, the instrument that sets the wheel in motion. The lengthy compound word that characterizes the wheel literally means "which revolves when touched by a series of strokes from the staff-tip of misfortune." The original Sanskrit holds the term in a compressed economy; there are no articles or prepositions to slow your perception.

Throughout India the body has been likened to a clay pot. For a short spell it holds the juices of life. Kabir (1398–1448?) sang of the body as a clay pot moistened with spit and semen. Broken, it returns to earth. Likewise Dadu Dayal, Kabir's contemporary, spoke of the pot with nine holes, wickedly asking, "Did you think it would last forever?" When a corpse has been consumed by fire on the burning *ghats* at Varanasi, a priest lifts a clay pot over his head and dashes it to pieces on the smoldering ash.

The word *vidhi*, best thought of here as fate or destiny, also means custom, convention, law. It is the name given to the Sanskrit subjunctive mode, *vidhi liṅ* (*liṅ* is a code-term referring to the verb). In English this would encompass the range of duty, conduct, hesitation, or excuse covered by *ought, should, could, would, might, may.* An underlying note therefore sounds through the poem: social expectation and prejudice are what "throw" one on the wheel.

"I should, I could, I ought, I would; I may have, I might have, I would have." These demands unhappily shape the poet, thrusting themselves between her life and her desires as the wheel revolves.

VIDYĀ

नीलोत्पलदलश्यामां विज्जिकां मामाजानता ।
वृथैव दण्डिना प्रोक्तं सर्वशुक्ला सरस्वती ॥
[PRM p46]

nīlotpaladalaśyāmāṃ vijjikāṃ māmājānatā
vṛthaiva daṇḍinā proktaṃ sarvaśuklā sarasvatī

nīla-utpala. blue lotus
dala. petal
śyāmāṃ. (f.) dark
vijjikāṃ. Vijjikā, or the poet Vidyā
māma. of me
ajānatā. (adj. with Dandin) not knowing, ignorant
vṛthā. falsely, frivolously
eva. indeed
daṇḍinā. by Dandin (a renowned critic)
proktaṃ. said, declared
sarva. entirely, completely, all
śuklā. white
sarasvatī. Sarasvatī, goddess of poetry, learning, and music

Not Knowing Me

Not knowing me,
Vidyā,
dark as a blue lotus petal,
the critic Dandin
declared our goddess of verse-craft and learning
  entirely white.

The verse from Dandin reads, *nityaṃ sarvaśuklā sarasvatī:* Sarasvatī eternally (or entirely) white. Sarasvatī is the *devī* who presides over poetry, music, and scholarship; her name means She-Who-Flows, as language and music flow through time. Her iconography typically depicts her features and clothing as white.

Little information on Vidyā is reliable. Based on this verse, some critics suggest she lived in the south of India, where complexions tend to be darker and skintones can have a blue cast. She has been called the Sarasvatī of Karnataka, a state in India's southeast.

Is the poem boastful? It is hard for me to see why Vidyā would bother to flaunt a dark (*śyāmā*) coloring, even if it is a splendid floral blue (*nīla*) associated with Krishna. I wonder if she's not delivering a deeper rebuke to the critic. For those who think careful craftsmanship, adherence to rules of grammar and metrics, and a classically trained use of adornments make poetry, Vidyā could be declaring that poems also emerge from troubled wells of experience, and are not simply those that are unstained. (*Śuklā*, a common woman's name, also means pure or unsullied.) Ruptures in language or violations of convention—such as Vidyā's mixing religious, erotic, and funerary language—would be part of the poet's work: twilight speech. Unfortunately only thirty of her lyrics survive, collected into anthologies long after her time—not enough for us to gauge the dimensions of her life, under what conditions she wrote, or how much.

तेषां गोपवधूविलाससुहृदां राधारहःसाक्षिणां
क्षेमं भद्र कलिन्दशैलतनयातीरे लतावेश्मनाम् ।
विच्छिन्ने स्मरतल्पकल्पनमृदुच्छेदोपयोगेऽधुना
ते जाने जरठीभवन्ति विगलन्नीलत्विषः पल्लवाः ।।

teṣām gopavadhūvilāsasuhṛdāṃ rādhārahaḥsākśiṇāṃ
kṣemaṃ bhadra kalindaśailatanayātīre latāveśmanām
vicchinne smaratalpakalpanamṛducchedopayoge 'dhunā
te jāne jaraṭhī bhavanti vigalannīlatviṣaḥ pallavāḥ

teṣāṃ. those
gopa-vadhū-vilāsa-suhṛdāṃ. (bv. cmpd. with vine-groves)
gopa-vadhū. cowherd's wife
vilāsa. passion, seduction, erotic desire
suhṛdāṃ. love, love-play
rādhā-rahaḥ-sākṣiṇāṃ. (bv. cmpd. for bowers: witnesses to secret affairs of Radha)
rahaḥ. secret
sākṣiṇāṃ. viewers, witnesses (literally, with eyes)
kṣemaṃ. prosperous, safe
bhadra. blessed, auspicious
kalinda-śaila. Kalinda Mountain
tanayā-tīre. daughter riverbank
tanayā. child, offspring (I think it means the bank is the descendant of Kalinda Mountain)
tīre. riverbank
latā-veśmanām. vine-groves, bowers or dwellings
vicchinne. (loc.) cut, torn, split
smara. love
talpa. bed
kalpana. arranged, made, fashioned
mṛdu. tender, pliant, soft
ccheda. cut
upayoge. enjoyment, love
adhunā. now, today
te. those (*pallavāḥ,* flowers)
jāne. I know (wonder)
jaraṭhī. bent, drooping, yellowed
bhavanti. (have they) become
vigala. dried up
nīla. dark blue
tviṣaḥ. splendor, beauty
pallavāḥ. buds, blossoms, shoots

And What of Those Arbors

And what of those
arbors of vines
that grow where the river
drops away from Kalinda Mountain?
They conspired in the love
games of herding girls
and watched over the veiled
affairs of Radha.
Now that the days
are gone when I cut their
tendrils, and laid them
down for couches of love,
I wonder if they've
grown brittle and if
their splendid blue flowers
have dried up.

If early dates for Vidyā are correct—around the seventh century—then this would be one of the first moments Radha steps from shadowy origins into poetry. Vidyā brings her onstage, confident that readers will know the story: that Radha is the cowherd girl beloved by Krishna, that their love goes through painful dark nights of separation, that their erotic union mirrors the human spirit's approach to divine wholeness. In Sanskrit poetry, the full account would appear in Jayadeva's *Gīta-Govinda* (twelfth century).

Vidyā's poem shows that the changing phases of Krishna and Radha's love were known to poets long before Jayadeva wrote. The late Barbara Miller, a fine scholar of Sanskrit, has traced Radha's name from its use for a two-star constellation in the sky (a force of nature) to its transference on Earth to this particular woman. Miller also suggests Vidyā's poem here may be in Radha's voice.

Yet the speaker sounds far removed from her youth, wistful for days long past or nights of love. The river is the Yāmunā (now Jumna), identified with Krishna's biogeography. Kalinda Mountain forms the backdrop—the watershed—for Krishna's *rasa-līlā,* or circle dance.

Vidyā calls the riverbank *tanayā*, daughter, of the mountain; another name for the river in India's sacred geography is Kalindī. An arbor or bower in the woods is where

Krishna and Radha first consummated their love, on a bed of flowered cuttings. The flowers are *nīla*, dark blue, a color sometimes associated with Krishna. It is also the color to which Vidyā likens her own complexion in her poem "Not Knowing Me."

The story of Radha may have been common property, circulated through villages by storytellers, dancers, puppeteers, theologians. But the emotion here is all Vidyā's.

FROM A POEM AT THE RIGHT MOMENT

Anonymous

संगीतं साहित्यं च सरस्वत्याः स्तनद्वयम् ।
एकमापातमधुरमन्यदालोचनामृतम् ॥

[PRM p61]

saṃgītaṃ sāhityaṃ ca sarasvatyāḥ stanadvayam
ekam āpātamadhuram anyad ālocanāmṛtam

saṃgītaṃ. music
sāhityaṃ. poetry, literature
ca. and
sarasvatyāḥ. (poss.) Sarasvatī has
stana. breasts
dvayam. two, a pair
ekam. one
āpāta. (*ā-pat,* fall downwards) instantly, readily
madhuram. sweet, honeyed
anyad. the other
ālocana. (by means of, through) reflecting, considering, looking over carefully, ruminating
amṛtam. ambrosia (is had)

Music and Poetry

Music and poetry,
Sarasvatī has two breasts
One's sweet at first sip—
the other, well, you need to
chew it a while

Sarasvatī presides over two arts. Music, the first, is enviably direct. Children, animals, even plants, respond to it instantly. By contrast, poetry is a more cultivated art; it demands solitary work and study. In classical India, the *sahṛdaya,* the person "with heart," spent a lifetime preparing for the poem. To the poet there's no doubt which art requires more sacrifice. Does arduous commitment on the part of poet and reader lead to immortality? Notice that music gives a quick earthy sweetness: *madhuram,* honeyed. Poetry, however—after *ālocana,* rumination—yields *amṛta,* the milk of deathlessness.

शापान्तो मे भुजगशयनादुत्थिते शार्ङ्गपाणौ
    शेषान्मासान्गमय चतुरो लोचने मीलयित्वा ।
पश्चादावां विरहगुणितं तं तमात्माभिलाषं
    निर्वेक्ष्यावः परिणतशरच्चन्द्रिकासु क्षपासु ॥

[MD 107]

śāpānto me bhujagaśayanād utthite śārṅgapāṇau
    śeṣānmāsān gamaya caturo locane mīlayitvā
paścād āvāṃ virahaguṇitaṃ taṃ tam ātmābhilāṣaṃ
    nirvekṣyāvaḥ pariṇataśaraccandrikāsu kṣapāsu

śāpa-anto. (at) curse's end
me. my
bhujaga. serpent
śayanāt. from a couch or bed
utthite. (is) when he rises
śārṅga-pāṇau. Vishnu, "armed with a bow"
śeṣān-māsān. remaining months
gamaya. (second-person imp.) cause to go past, permit to pass
caturo. four (with months)
locane. (your two) eyes
mīlayitvā. having closed
paścād. afterwards
āvāṃ. our
viraha. separation
guṇitaṃ. completed
taṃ tam. this and that (those)
ātma-abhilāṣaṃ. our desires
nirvekṣyāvaḥ. we will enjoy, release, settle (as in a payment)
pariṇata-śarat-candrikāsu. (bv. cmpd. with *kṣapāsu*) at the time of the full autumn moon
pariṇata. full, ripe
śarat. autumn
candrikāsu. moon
kṣapāsu. during the hours, twenty-four hours, a day

The Curse Upon Me

The curse upon me ends
when Vishnu
rises from his serpent bed.
Close your eyes, let
the four remaining months
drift past. Then
all those desires
ripened by separation
we'll slake at night
beneath the huge harvest moon.

In Kālidāsa's poem of 111 stanzas, *Meghadūta*, the lovers have fallen under a curse. Exile will separate them through the rainy months, the period of the year when Vishnu sleeps on the coils of a cosmic serpent.

Kālidāsa has hidden a notable pun here. The *śeṣān-māsān* (remaining months) are also the serpent months. *Śeṣa* means snake or serpent, but originally refers to the snake's sloughed skin. The word thus means remainder, leftover, the slough. The opening lines of this stanza are astronomical and refer to the night sky. In autumn Vishnu, *śārṅga-pāṇi* (holder of the horn-bow) wakens or rises above the horizon, coinciding with the appearance of both harvest and hunter's moons. Similarly, in Occidental astronomy, the hunter Orion becomes vivid in the Northern Hemisphere's night sky with the onset of autumn. A nearly universal language of symbols links poets across Eurasia and the Americas, many of these symbols traceable to archaic hunting cultures.

Recent studies of vocabulary spanning the Northern Hemisphere have some linguists proposing a distant ancestral language they call proto-Eurasian, dating back 15,000 years, to the last "glacial maximum" or Ice Age. Comparing words for mother, milk, and a few other extremely common terms that apparently change very slowly over time, they think they've found evidence that the most wide-flung languages have a kinship that began when the caves at Lascaux were being painted. I suspect that only slightly less basic would be vivid words like serpent, archer, moon, love. If a single archaic language did stretch through Europe, across the width of Asia, over the Bering Strait, to where the Inuit live—the range proposed for this proto-Eurasian tongue—a poem like this verse of Kālidāsa's might offer a glimpse into its songs.

रम्याणि वीक्ष्य मधुरांश्च निशम्य शब्दान्
पर्युत्सुको भवति यत्सुखितोऽपि जन्तुः ।
तच्चेतसा स्मरति नूनमबोधपूर्वं
भावस्थिराणि जननान्तरसौहृदानि ॥

[AS]

ramyāṇi vīkṣya madhurāṃś ca niśamya śabdān
paryutsuko bhavati yat sukhito'pi jantuḥ
tac cetasā smarati nūnam abhodha pūrvaṃ
bhāvasthirāṇi jananāntarasauhṛdāni

ramyāṇi. beauties, beautiful objects
vīkṣya. having seen
madhurāṃ. sweet, honeyed
ca. and
niśamya. having heard
śabdān. sounds
paryutsuko. (bv. cmpd.) restless, stricken
bhavati. becomes
yat. he who
sukhito. content, happy
'pi. (api) even
jantuḥ. man, person
tat-cetasā. with his heart
smarati. remembers
nūnam. now (here: perhaps)
abodha. without knowing
pūrvaṃ. previously, long ago
bhāva. emotions
sthirāṇi. stationed, established
janana-antara. (of a) former lifetime
sauhṛdāni. loves, companions

Looking at Well-Crafted Objects

Looking at well-crafted objects
hearing sweet music
even the contented person
grows edgy
pierced by unknown desires.
Could it be deep
in the heart one uncovers
the trace of a lover
from lifetimes ago?

This poem occurs in Kālidāsa's dramatic work *The Recollection of Śakuntalā*. Indian poets and critics have cited it for centuries, using it to get to the heart of *rasa*.

In the play, a young warlord on a hunting expedition encounters a girl, Śakuntalā, who has been raised in a cloistered forest ashram by her mendicant father. Prince and girl fall for each other and consummate their love in a wooded glade. By India's old conventions, this is a "*gandharva* wedding"—a ceremony sanctified by the *gandharvas*, celestial musicians who watch over human love. The young couple strolls through the woods after their lovemaking and literally trip across a severe recluse, disrupting his meditation. In a fit of rage, the powerful *yogin* hurls a curse: when the prince returns home, no matter his vows, all memory of Śakuntalā will be obliterated.

In a subsequent scene, the warlord is back in his life of wealth and rank when he hears a strain of music drift through the palace. A former lover of his plays on a musical instrument in her far-off quarters, the song a subtle reproach for his neglect of her. His heart, unexpectedly pierced, becomes *paryutsuka*, troubled, full of longing, brimming with uncertain desire and regret. The audience knows that a trace of Śakuntalā, some thin strand of passion, runs through his body, too buried by the curse to rise into consciousness. It is at this moment in the play—most likely accompanied by ceremonial dance—he recites, *ramyāṇi vīkṣya* . . .

For poets, the stanza is the perfect isolation of *rasa*, bedrock emotional territory that underlies our surface passions. The purpose of poetry is to access that subconscious material, to provide a "taste" of the underlying white-hot encounter with what's real. To the philosopher this taste is a "foretaste" of spiritual liberation.

Most Indian accounts of the origins or the purpose of art have proceeded from the concept of *rasa*, ever since the Kashmiri poet-philosopher Abhinavagupta set down its metaphysical basis in the tenth- or eleventh-century treatise *Abhinavabhāratī*. The eight (or at times nine or ten) *rasas* are the names of emotional states: erotic love, humor, grief, rage, revulsion, horror, heroism, and wonder. Laid out in a visual psychology, each has a color, a direction, a deity, a time of day or year, and many other associations. Originally meaning juice, sap, semen, *rasa* came to mean the essence or life-juice of anything, its "taste." René Daumal translated *rasa* as *saveur*.

The questions raised by this poem edge into psychoanalysis, evolutionary biology, and ecology. What is the wild unnamed edginess a person approaches in art? Why should things of beauty provoke desire instead of allay it? How far does memory reach, and through it do we actually touch other persons? How is art able to make us feel as though we've brushed against former life memories?

The poem uses technical terms hard to match closely in English. *Ramyāṇi* are things that are gorgeous because they provoke bodily desire, from the verbal root *ram*, to make love. The *bhāva-sthirāṇi* are deep-seated personal emotions—almost "complexes"—at the core of the individual. *Janana-antara* are previous lifetimes. I think the belief is that *bhāva-sthirāṇi* are what carry from one life to another. Bundled together they form the soul of a person, the "shape of a life." Or they comprise the husk of passions that sheathes the spirit.

KĀLIDĀSA

कमले कमलोत्पत्तिः श्रूयते न च दृश्यते ।
बाले तव मुखाम्भोजे कथं इन्दीवरद्वयम् ॥

kamale kamalotpattiḥ śrūyate na ca dṛśyate
bāle tava mukhāmbhoje kathaṃ indīvaradvayaṃ

kamale. on a lotus
kamala-utpattiḥ. the emergence of a lotus
śrūyate. is heard
na. not
ca. and, however
dṛśyate. is seen
bāle. (voc.) young woman
tava. your
mukha-ambho-je. on the water-born face
(several white lotuses are called *ambhoja,* water born)
kathaṃ. how
indīvara. small blue lotus or day lily
dvayam. two, a pair

Death Poem

"A lotus born from a lotus"
    heard of but not seen.
Girl, on your waterborn-lotus-face
    how are there two indigo lotuses?

Rāja Kumāradāsa, known for his allegiance to poetry, wrote a couplet, the first half of this stanza, on the wall of a courtesan's quarters, and offered a reward to whoever could finish the poem; the opening phrase may have been a familiar maxim on the South Asian subcontinent. Underneath Kumāradāsa's lines, his friend Kālidāsa provided the second couplet, completing the poem.

Not much of a poem by any standard. But the stakes were high, and Kālidāsa's lines proved his undoing. Hungry for the king's reward, the courtesan in whose quarters he wrote it poisoned Kālidāsa. She presented the verse as her own. Kumāradāsa, however, was undeceived. He recognized the hand of his friend and forced the truth from her. Then, stricken at the loss of his court poet and dearest friend, the king cast himself on Kālidāsa's funeral pyre.

Evidence exists of a pan-Asian tradition of poetry contests in which the opening half of a poem is put up for public display. I'd be surprised if the practice doesn't go back to archaic oral traditions. Certain Himalayan villages hold courtship events where girls and boys eagerly compete to outdo each other with improvised sexual riddle-poems. The Japanese practice of *renga* (linked verse), widespread from the sixteenth century on, is a type of high-culture poetry contest for literate people.

Probably the most celebrated poem-on-wall contest occurs in the Chinese *Platform Sutra*, a central Zen text. The Fifth Patriarch, Hung-jen, challenged his disciples to write a *gāthā* (devotion verse) on the monastery wall, telling his students that whoever showed the profoundest insight would receive transmission and inherit the robe, bowl, and staff of the Dharma. Senior practice instructor Shen-Hsiu went to the wall and wrote

The body is a bodhi tree
the mind is like a standing mirror
always try to keep it clean
don't let it gather dust.

None of the other senior monks dared a verse of his own. The novice Hui Neng, the kitchen dishwasher and lowest of the monastery's residents, heard talk of the verse and went at night to study it. Illiterate, he had to have a friend read it to him by torchlight.

Instantly recognizing its flawed insight, he recited another poem, which his companion wrote underneath:

> The mind is the bodhi tree
> the body is the mirror's stand
> the mirror itself is so clean
> dust has no place to land.
>
> *Translated by Red Pine*

Jealousy factors into this story, as it did in Kālidāsa's. Receiving transmission and the treasures of Buddhist insight from the monastery's teacher, Hui Neng flees by night into the wilderness to escape the murderous envy that arises among the long-term disciples. One ruffian even chases him up a snow-covered mountain pass.

The underlying theme—poem-on-a-wall contest—may well be a worldwide folklore motif, an instance of "archaic internationalism," as Gary Snyder calls it. In post-archaic times in India and China, winners were handsomely rewarded.

Ambho-ja is any of several large white or day lotuses; the Sanskrit means water born. The *indīvara* is the smaller blue lotus or blue water lily *(Nymphaea stellata).*

Curiously, the *indīvara* (blue lotus) of Kālidāsa's poem, is also a Buddhist symbol. The national flower of both Sri Lanka and Bangladesh, it is said to have bloomed wherever Buddha walked. The poem stands in India as Kālidāsa's death song.

समदिवसनिशीथं संगिनस्तत्र शम्भोः
शतमगमदृतूनां साग्रमेका निशैव ।
न तु सुरतसुखेभ्यश्छिन्नतृष्णो बभूव
ज्वलन इव समुद्रान्तर्गतस्तज्जलेषु ॥
[KS]

samadivasaniśītham̧ saṅginas tatra śambhoḥ
śatam agamad ṛtūnām̧ sāgramekā niśaiva
na tu suratasukhebhyaś chinnatṛṣṇo babhūva
jvalana iva samudrāntargatas taj jaleṣu

sama. same
divasa. day
niśītham̧. night
saṅginas. united with, absorbed
tatra. there
śambhoḥ. Śiva the beneficent
śatam. hundred
agamad. went
ṛtūnām̧. of seasons
sa. he
agram-ekā. one single, just one
niśā. night
eva. as though
na [and] *chinna.* not cut off, not abated
tu. but
surata. lovemaking
sukhebhyaḥ. delights
chinna-tṛṣṇo. (person with) abated thirst
babhūva. was
jvalana. fire
iva. just as
samudrā. ocean
antar-gataḥ. gone under
taj. (for *tat*) that
jaleṣu. in the waters

Absorbed Night and Day

Absorbed night and day
Śiva makes love
to Pārvatī
his hunger for pleasure
not slaked.
Like a single night
a hundred aeons
roll past.
In ocean's deep waters
slow geomorphic flames twist
they too
unabated.

Only eight cantos of Kālidāsa's long poem *Kumārasambhava* (The Birth of Kumāra) come down to us. The poem's leisurely narrative never reaches the birth, let alone the deeds, of the prince of war, Śiva's son. The book leaves off in the midst of Śiva's rapture with his mountain-girl bride, Pārvatī, daughter of the Himālaya. The poem's narrative, told from multiple perspectives, is a sustained study in desire, and Kālidāsa depicts love as the generative force of the cosmos. This verse closes the eighth canto.

Scholars surmise that Kālidāsa died midway through the writing of *Kumārasambhava.* I find it tempting to think that this, then, is the last verse he wrote. As a death poem, it is entirely more satisfying than the "two blue lotuses" that legend assigns him. This verse offers a vision of a mutable world of molten force, animated by love, moving at a geological pace and spanning reaches of time no human can quite comprehend. If human love responds to and is mirrored by plants, animals, flowers, breezes, and rain on Earth's surface, it seems fitting that the gods should make love in the massive, underlying metamorphic forces of Earth. Their love takes place in geological time: a hundred seasons or aeons (*ṛtu* means both) leave their desire unquenched.

In *mahākāvya* (long poems) individual verses accrue to shape a narrative. At the same time, each is composed to stand on its own, apart from its original context. This one, I like to imagine, finishes Kālidāsa's poem; in it he views his own death from the long, cool perspective of Deep Time.

HASTIPAKA

अम्भोमुचां सलिलमुद्गिरतां निशिथे
ताडीवनेषु निभृतस्थितकर्णतालाः ।
आकर्णयन्ति करिनोऽर्धनिमीलिताक्षा
धाराखं दशनकोटिनिषण्णहस्ताः ॥
[SR 1161]

ambhomucāṃ salilamudgiratāṃ niśithe
tāḍīvaneṣu nibhṛtasthitakarṇatālāḥ
ākarṇayanti karino'rdhanimīlitākṣā
dhārāravaṃ daśanakoṭiniṣaṇṇahastāḥ

ambho-mucāṃ. (bv. cmpd.)
water-releasers (clouds)
salilam-udgiratāṃ. (bv. cmpd.)
rain-dischargers (clouds)
niśithe. in the night
tāḍī. toddy palms
vaneṣu. in the groves
nibhṛtasthitakarṇatālāḥ. (bv. cmpd.)
the ones standing hidden who
beat their ears
nibhṛta. hidden
sthita. standing
karṇa. ears
tālāḥ. rhythm (beat)
ākarṇayanti. (they) listen
karinaḥ. elephants
'rdhanimīlitākṣā. (bv. cmpd.)
'rdha. half
nimīlita. closed
ākṣā. eyes
dhārā. rain
ravaṃ. roar
daśanakoṭiniṣaṇṇahastāḥ. (bv. cmpd.)
daśana. tusk
koṭi. tips
niṣaṇṇa. settled, resting
hastāḥ. trunks

Rain Slants Steadily

Rain slants steadily
through the night-bound
toddy-palm forest.
Concealed by huge fronds
the elephants,
eyes half open,
        ears beating a slow rhythm and trunks
slung over their tusk-tips,
listen to the unbroken
downpour.

Nothing is known of Hastipaka, to whom the poem is attributed. The name means elephant keeper, mahout. No other poems show up with this name. In this sense, it might be an honorary title more than a name, speaking to the poem's masterful imagery. The common Sanskrit terms for elephant refer to its trunk. *Karin,* in this poem, and *hastin,* both mean "having a hand," references to the trunk's dexterity. In Rudyard Kipling's *The Jungle Book* and in the animated Disney film based on it, the king elephant's name is Hatha, a modern Hindustani derivative.

At one level the poem is a crisp snapshot of natural history. What a gripping detail: how the elephants sling their trunks over their tusk tips—a gesture that contrasts with their ears, which are *tālāḥ* (beating a rhythm). *Tāla* is the technical term for rhythmic cycles in Indian music, which the drummer establishes.

The anthology the poem appears in was compiled by Vidyākara, abbot of the Buddhist monastery of Jagaddala, in Bengal. It might be that one could add a second reading to the poem: it shows the meditative tranquility of the elephant—an image regularly used for the Buddha (or Buddha mind) in sculpture, friezes, and paintings. Was the poem iconic? Meant to invoke the buddhas, to depict wandering monks waiting out the rains in a forest retreat, or to embody a state of mind? To enter its cadence might be to enter a *samādhi,* the calm vigilance of elephant mind.

I'll take the poem through one other realm. In ancient India a sympathetic magic held between elephants and rain clouds, a discussion of which appears in Heinrich Zimmer's *Myths and Symbols in Indian Art and Civilization.* Elephants were once clouds, able to roam the skies. After an angry ascetic "grounded" a herd, humans saw elephants as close kin to the monsoon storm clouds, the *ambho-mucāṃ* (water-dischargers) of the poem. When a kingdom suffered drought in ancient times, an elephant would be brought to court to lure rain.

If it refers to the kinship between elephants and rain, the origins of this poem, then, could have been spells, by which specialists (rainmakers) manipulated or conjured weather. Oral formulas might not require an elephant be present, only the right words. Evoking the necessary images through recitation or incantation would be enough. In that sense, the poet here is like a duck hunter who doesn't need a decoy—he only needs to reproduce the mallard's call.

उद्वृत्तस्तनभार एष तरले नेत्रे चले भ्रूलते
रागाधिक्यतम् ओष्ठपल्लवदलं कुर्वन्तु नाम व्यथाम् ।
सौभाग्याक्षरपंक्तिकेव लिखिता पुष्पायुधेन स्वयं
मध्यस्था हि करोति तापमधिकं रोमावली केन सा ॥

[119]

udvṛttastanabhāra eṣa tarale netre cale bhrūlate
rāgādhikyatam oṣṭhapallavadalaṃ kurvantu nāma vyathām
saubhāgyākṣarapaṃktikeva likhitā puṣpāyudhena svayaṃ
madhyasthā hi karoti tāpam adhikaṃ romāvalī kena sā

udvṛtta. uplifted
stana-bhāra. breasts
eṣa. this
tarale. flashing, quick
netre. eyes
cale. moving
bhrūlate. eyebrows
rāga-ādhikyatam. passionate
oṣṭha-palla-vadalaṃ. lips like flowerbuds
kurvantu. let them make
nāma. surely
vyathām. unease, distress (for me)
saubhāgya-akṣara-paṅktikā. (bv. cmpd. with *romāvalī*) gorgeous imperishable line
saubhāgya. beauty, charm
akṣara. imperishable, unforgettable
paṅktikā. a line, a meter
iva. like
likhitā. written, inscribed
puṣpā-yudhena. by the flowerlike bow (of love)
svayaṃ. her
madhyasthā. belly or navel
hi. surely
karoti. makes
tāpam. torment, anguish
adhikaṃ. excessive, much
romāvalī. line of hair above the pubis
kena sā. why, how

Her Quick Eyes

Her quick eyes
and animated mouth
unsettle me.
So, of course,
her lifted breasts,
full lips—
soft fruits of desire.
But why should a
single wisp of hair,
stroked beneath her
navel like
some unforgettable
line of poetry,
reduce me to such
anguish?

Saubhāgya-akṣara-paṅktikā means a splendid or gorgeously imperishable poetic line. A pun may lie hidden in *saubhāgya*, referring to the vulva, adding to the poet's charged emotion. The poetic line is literally stroked by the bow (with flower-tipped arrows of Kāma, desire). The image is conventional enough in Sanskrit poetry; nobody would really notice. But in English I thought it would call too much attention to itself and distract from Bhartṛhari's intent.

The *romāvalī* (line of hair running from the navel down) was regarded by Indian poets as a particularly enticing mark of beauty. The word for anguish, *tāpam,* means heat, fever; it is also the term in spiritual traditions for ascetic practice. Bhartṛhari's poetry is always torn between *vairāgya* (renunciation) and *śṛṅgāra* (erotic pleasure). Two of his three collections of poetry have been given those titles.

यत्रानेकः क्वचिदपि गृहे तत्र तिष्ठत्यथैको
    यत्रापि एकस्तदनु बहवस्तत्र चान्ते न चैकः ।
इत्थं चेमौ रजनिदिवसौ दोलयन्द्वाविवाक्षौ
    कालः काल्या सह बहुकलः क्रीदति प्राणिसारैः ॥

[171]

yatrānekaḥ kvacid api gṛhe tatra tiṣṭhatyathaiko
    yatrāpi ekastadanu bahavas tatra cānte na caikaḥ
ittham cemau rajanidivasau dolayan dvāvivākṣau
    kālaḥ kālyā saha bahukalaḥ krīdati prāṇisāraiḥ

yatra. where
anekaḥ. many (none were solitary)
kvacit. people
api. once (were)
gṛhe. in a house, mansion
tatra. there
tiṣṭhati. stands
atha. now
eko. one alone
yatra-api. in fact where
ekas-tadanu. descendants
bahavaḥ. many
tatra. there were
ca-ante. now at the end
na ca. not
ekaḥ. one
ittham. thus, in this way
ca. and
imau. two people
rajani-divasau. night and day
dolayan. tossing
dvau. two
iva. like
akṣau. dice, pawns, gambling items
kālaḥ. Time
kālyā-saha. with Kālī
bahukalaḥ. intensely, fiercely
krīdati. plays
prāṇisāraiḥ. at destruction, extinction

In a Mansion

In a mansion
where once many dwelt
a single man stands.
Where countless descendants thronged
at the last count
no one remains.
Tossing day and night
like dice
toppling people like pawns,
Time plays with Kālī
the game of ultimate extinction.

The original holds the tossing of dice and the toppling of pawns in a single image. A reader of Sanskrit sees them simultaneously. Kālī is the black goddess, the one who devours her children; she and Kāla (time) play the endgame, *bahukala* (fiercely or repeatedly), filling the poem's fourth line with the syllables *kā* and *la.*

To get at Bhartṛhari's troubled temperament, this poem should be paired with the preceding one. The legend of the seventh-century poet has him tormented equally by a life of worldly, sensuous pleasures and by the hermit's cool-tempered solitude in the forest. In the world, death and destruction lie just beneath his pleasures; in the woods, he cannot shake sexual hunger or the grinding onset of old age. Legend says that, unable to choose a course, he swung seven times between the two lifestyles.

Eventually, Bhartṛhari fell in love with a woman at court and presented her a magical amulet. She loved another man, though, and gave the amulet to him. This man, yearning for a different woman at court, gave the treasure to her. To complete the cycle, this second woman secretly longed for Bhartṛhari, and returned the treasure to him. He stood contemplating the cycle of thwarted desire, vanity, and ignorance, and departed to the forest for good.

The Tang Dynasty Chinese pilgrim Hsuan-tsang, who visited India in search of Buddhist manuscripts, heard of the poet, and wrote of him as a Buddhist. The poems show Buddhist sensibility—everything's impermanent—but also invoke Hindu deities. One verse says, *mohaṃ marjāya upārjaya ratiṃ candrārdhacūḍāmanau:* "Purge delusion, take pleasure through Śiva, who wears the crescent moon in his hair."

भ्रातः कष्टमहो महान् स नृपतिः सामन्तचक्रं च तत्
पार्श्वे तस्य च सापि राजपरिषत्ताश्चन्द्रबिम्बाननाः ।
उद्रिक्तः स च राजपुत्रनिवहस्ते बन्दिनस्ताः कथाः
सर्वं यस्य वशादगात् स्मृतिपदं कालाय तस्मै नमः ॥

[169]

bhrātaḥ kaṣṭamaho mahān sa nṛpatiḥ sāmantacakraṃ ca tat
pārśve tasya ca sāpi rājapariṣat tāś candrabimbānanāḥ
udriktaḥ sa ca rājaputranivahas te bandinas tāḥ kathāḥ
sarvaṃ yasya vaśād agāt smṛtipadaṃ kālāya tasmai namaḥ

bhrātaḥ. (voc.) Oh brother
kaṣṭam. grief
aho. [cry of grief]
mahān. great
sa nṛpatiḥ. the king
sāmanta-cakraṃ. inner circle (courtiers)
ca tat. with
pārśve. at (his) flank
tasya. his
ca. and
sa api. also
rāja-pariṣat. council of advisors
tāḥ candra-bimba-ananāḥ. (bv. cmpd.) the moon-disc-face-ones (women)
udriktaḥ. prominent (adj. with warlords)
sa ca. and the
rāja-putra-nivahaḥ. multitude of warlords *(rājaputra)*
te bandinaḥ. the poets or heralds who praise the king
tāḥ kathāḥ. their chronicles
sarvaṃ. all
yasya. of this
vaśat. from power
agāt. gone, swept
smṛti-padaṃ. into memory (literally, onto the path of memory)
kālāya. by Time
tasmai. to whom
namaḥ. homage (we bow)

Grieve, Brother!

Grieve, brother!
Great was the king with his
inner circle,
a council that flanked him,
warlords in prominent ranks,
courtesans pale as moonlight.
Scribes and poets
chronicled it all as it happened.
Those days have vanished
swept into memory
by Time—
to whom we
finally kneel down.

This poem reminds me of another, from the anthology *Sattasai* (Seven Hundred Poems of Hāla). Tradition places that book two thousand years before the present, and therefore six hundred years earlier than Bhatṛhari's poem. Bhartṛhari's has a wide sweep—the deep gong of prophecy—while the earlier poem, written in a vernacular of Maharashtra State, rings with an acutely personal grief over time's passage.

Young Men

Young men
used to slip this
wooden Ganesh
under my head for a pillow
today
cursing old age
I bow down before it

[Anonymous, *Sattasai* 4:72]

Translated by Andrew Schelling

जयन्ति ते सुकृतिनो
        रससिद्धाः कवीश्वराः ।
नास्ति येषां यशःकाये
        जरामरणजन्मभिः ॥
[55]

jayanti te sukṛtino
        rasasiddhāḥ kavīśvarāḥ
nāsti yeṣāṃ yaśaḥkāye
        jarāmaraṇajanmabhiḥ

jayanti. triumph
te. they
sukṛtino. accomplished, cultivated
rasa. [see pages 43–44 for discussion of this term]
siddhāḥ. wizards, shamans, spiritual masters
kavi-iśvarāḥ. poet-masters
na-asti. is no
yeṣāṃ. for them
yaśaḥ. of splendor, glory, fame
kāye. in the body
jarā-maraṇa-janmabhiḥ. old age, death, rebirth

Victory

Victory to
the accomplished master poets
wizards of *rasa*—
in their bodies of splendor they suffer
no old age no death
no rebirth.

Rasas are what John Cage calls the "permanent emotions." In Indian metaphysics they are *alokita,* not located anywhere. It is our mutable emotions that consume us and have a nameable location, attached to one object or another. They dissolve when our bodies die. *Rasas* underlie the passions, a vast substratum or territory that emotion arises from and that is accessed through art. In fact that would be the purpose of art: to reach into that unconscious realm.

Bhatṛhari speaks of poets as *rasa-siddhas.* A *siddha* is a spiritual adept. Different traditions of yoga or Buddhist practice inflect the term differently. The root verb, *sidh,* simply means to accomplish, and *siddha* means one-who-has-accomplished or reached mastery. You could call *siddhas* shamans, wizards, enlightened ones. In their bodies of *yaśa* (brilliance, glory, or fame), they escape the perilous wheel of birth and death.

Bhartṛhari did not consider poetry something separate from spiritual practice; through it, the person who achieves mastery attains liberation. Contrast this with Viśvanātha's invocation in "Shining with the Luster." On one path, the poet approaches Language as a power greater than himself, as a goddess, and prays for her to succeed. On another path, Bhartṛhari sees the poet achieving enlightenment through his or her own hard-earned accomplishment.

विलासमसृणोल्लसन्मुसललोलदोःकन्दली-
परस्परपरिस्खलद्वलयनिःस्वनैर्दन्तुराः ।
हरन्ति कलहूंकृतिप्रसभकम्पितोरःसथल-
त्रुटद्गमकसंकुलाः कलमकण्डनीगीतयः ॥
[SR 1178]

vilāsamasṛṇollasanmusalaloladoḥkandalī-
parasparapariskhaladvalayaniḥsvanair danturāḥ
haranti kalahūṃkṛtiprasabhakampitoraḥsathala-
truṭadgamakasaṃkulāḥ kalamakaṇḍanīgītayaḥ

vilāsa. teasing, seductive
masṛṇa. tender, smooth
ullasat. rising, bright
musala. rice pestle
lola. dangling, swinging to and fro
doḥ. arm, forearm
kandalī. bracelets
paraspara. one another
pariskhala. clanging, ringing against
niḥsvanair. with sharp sounds
danturāḥ. interspersed, alternating
haranti. they (the songs) seize, are gripping
kala. low, soft
hūṃkṛti. hum, groan
prasabha. fiercely, violently
kampita. heaving, trembling
uraḥ. breasts
sa-thala-truṭa. torn (from)
gamaka. deep tone, drone
saṃkulāḥ. accompanied by
kalama-kaṇḍanī. (bv. cmpd.) rice mortar (women)
gītayaḥ. songs

They Seize One's Heart

They seize one's heart
these rice-husking
songs of the women—
bracelets chiming
along their bare arms
as they swing
the glistening rice paddles.
Teasing, tender,
now teasing again—
a low-toned *hum*
forced by exertion from
swaying breasts
underlies the singing
like a drone.

Thirty-eight poems by Yogeśvara come from the *Subhāṣitaratnakoṣa,* Vidyākara's eleventh-century collection. Daniel H. H. Ingalls, the Harvard University scholar who published a translation of the anthology in 1965, coined the term "school of forest and field" for a number of the poets from Bengal. Chief among these, he says, is Yogeśvara, who once wrote, "my heart belongs to the meadow by the bend in the river." Yogeśvara's poems come as a fresh breeze through field and forest, memorably portraying agricultural and hunting people.

Vilāsa-masṛṇa reminds me of Japanese poet Bashō's *haiku,* which suggests peasant rice-planting songs as the "origin of poetry." Yogeśvara does not say it explicitly, and as far as I know there's no evidence, but it seems his attraction to rural song and music comes from a similar instinct. The rice-husking songs are by turns *vilāsa* (seductive or playful) and *masṛṇa* (soothing or tender).

Two long compounds describe the songs: they are "alternately seductive & tender punctuated by sharp sounds from bracelets clanging &c." and are "accompanied by a low-toned *hūṃkṛti* torn from fiercely heaving breasts." Notice that the first two lines of Sanskrit form a single long compound, the sort of structure that gives the tradition astounding compression. "Minimum words, maximum meaning," Allen Ginsberg would say. Poets would often—as Yogeśvara does here—build the compounds on repetition of sounds, believing that those particular sounds carry precise spiritual power and propel the listener into deep emotion, *rasa.*

आसारान्तमृदुप्रवृत्तमरुतो मेघोपलिप्ताम्बरा
विद्युत्पातमुहूर्तदृष्टककुभः सुप्तेन्दुताराग्रहाः ।
धाराक्लिन्नकदम्बसंभृतसुरामोदोद्वहाः प्रोषितैर्
निःसंपातविसारिदर्दुररवा नीताः कथं रात्रयः ॥
[SR 220]

āsārāntamṛdupravṛttamaruto meghopaliptāmbarā
vidyutpātamuhūrtadṛṣṭakakubhaḥ suptendutārāgrahāḥ
dhārāklinnakadambasaṃbhṛtasurāmododvahāḥ proṣitair
niḥsaṃpātavisāridardurаravā nītāḥ kathaṃ rātrayaḥ

āsārānta. a hard rain
mṛdu. soft, tender, gentle
pravṛtta. come forth, all around
maruto. wind
megha. clouds
upalipta. covered, overlaid
ambarā. sky
vidyut-pāta. lightning-flash
muhūrta. moment, instant
dṛṣṭa. seen
kakubhaḥ. horizon, quarter of the heavens
supta-indu-tārā-grahāḥ. (adj. with nights) gripped by sleeping moon and stars
supta. sleep
indu. moon
tārā. stars
grahāḥ. grasped, taken
dhārā. carrying, bearing
klinna. wet, moist
kadamba. a tree (*Neolamarckia cadamba*) with fragrant orange blossoms
saṃbhṛta. gathered, collected
surāmododvahāḥ. intoxicating fragrance
proṣitaiḥ. by a traveler; one absent or gone on a journey; the dead
niḥsampāta. thick darkness, depth of night
visāri. spread
dardura. frogs
ravā. noise, croak, roar
nītāḥ. are passed
kathaṃ. how
rātrayaḥ. nights (the long compounds describe the nights)

Hard Rain

Hard rain
then soft wind,
a sky smoking with clouds.
Flashes of lightning
stroke a horizon
that's there and then not there.
Moon and stars vanished,
fragrant wet flowers,
darkness creaking with frogs.
And a solitary traveler?
Can he get
through the nights?

Earth conspires in the erotic emotions, and the most acute form of eroticism is longing due to separation or absence. In the early Indic world, humans lived in direct relation to the natural orders, so the evocation of elemental or natural forces would be evocation of *rasa,* deep spirit. Do I detect in so many poems like this not just description, but traces of archaic speech-magic, which could summon the rains by invoking them? In *The Essential Haiku,* Robert Hass observes something comparable behind *haiku:* "My personal theory, not especially well-informed, about *kigo* [seasonal words] is that their origin is shamanic, animistic, and ritualistic, that the words . . . were intended at one time to call forth the living spirits manifested in those natural phenomena." As Hass notes, shaman songs passed into folk song.

In India the trained court poets regularly drew on folk-song models. They believed the earliest anthology of their tradition, the *Sattasai* of King Hāla, contained songs collected from rural villages and possibly tribes that lived by the hunt. Animist beliefs would leave tracks in the poetry. Of Sanskrit poets, Yogeśvara in particular had an ethnographer's eye and ear and traveled among tribal people who still ritualized their animist beliefs.

Proṣita, the word here for traveler, also refers to those gone on the long journey: the dead. The poem's structure is a single utterance, one sentence: "How are nights passed by a traveler?" Everything else is a compound word describing the nights, which are "clasped in the sleep [concealment] of moon and stars." So much detail and passion held in a single breath.

तैस्तैर्जीवोपहारैरिह कुहरशिलासंश्रयामर्चयित्वा
देवीं कान्तारदुर्गां रुधिरमुपतरु क्षेत्रपालाय दत्वा ।
तुम्बीवीणाविनोदव्यवहितसरकामह्नि जीर्णे पुराणीं
हालां मालूरकोषैर्युवतिसहचरा बर्बराः शीलयन्ति ॥

[SR 1191]

tais tair jīvopahārair iha kuharaśilāsaṃśrayām arcayitvā
devīṃ kāntāradurgāṃ rudhiramupataru kṣetrapālāya datvā
tumbīvīṇāvinodavyavahitasarakām ahni jīrṇe purāṇīṃ
hālāṃ mālūrakoṣair yuvatisahacarā barbarāḥ śīlayanti

taiḥ taiḥ. by them
jīva. of live creatures
upahāraiḥ. sacrifices, sacrifice of living beings
iha. here
kuhara. hollow
śilā. rock, crag
saṃśrayām. dwelling, sheltering
arcayitvā. praising
devīṃ. goddess
kāntāra-durgā. wilderness Durgā (the goddess in her most dangerous aspect)
rudhiram. of blood
upataru. draughts, sloshes
kṣetra-pālāya. to the "field-protector" or tree-spirit
datvā. giving
tumbī-vīṇā. gourd-lute
vinoda. sporting, playing
vyavahita. alternating, stopping and starting
sarakām. passing (the liquor) about
ahni. on festival day
jīrṇe. late (in the day)
purāṇīṃ. the old way, in the tradition
hālāṃ. liquor
mālūrakoṣaiḥ. in the *bilva*-fruit husk
yuvati-saha-carā. dancing with their women
barbarāḥ. tribesmen (see our English word "barbarian")
śīlayanti. repeatedly doing

The Tribesmen Dispatch

The tribesmen dispatch
creature after
living creature to Durgā,
goddess who dwells in a craggy wilderness grotto.
They slosh the blood on a field-spirit tree.
Then joined by their women at dusk
go wild to the gourd-lute
stopping just to pass liquor around—
the old way—
in a *bilva* fruit husk.

In addition to his ethnographer's eye, Yogeśvara had a constant hunger for locating early forms of music or song. His tone is even—not appalled at the sacrifice of animals, not alarmed by frenzy or hard drinking—quick to notice details such as the "old way" *(purāṇīṃ)* to pass drink around. The ceremony he describes still exists in remote parts of Eastern India, or did so until recently.

In 1993 a friend and I visited Gond tribal districts in Orissa State, a bit south of Yogeśvara's Bengal. Beyond the clustered, thatch-roofed village huts in the scrub jungle stood decorated spirit trees and stockades for sacrificing buffalo. Well-tramped tiny dance grounds lay in front of the stockades, and clay pots hung high off the trunks of the tall, thin toddy-palm trees. These collected the sap fermented for liquor. British authorities in the eighteenth and nineteenth centuries discouraged the rituals held next to the spirit trees but did not forbid them. In Orissa, missionaries tried to substitute Presbyterian churches for the ancient church of field and forest, but had limited success. The "old ways" ceremonies still take place, but wary tribal people melt away when outsiders arrive. Visitors seem less welcome than in Yogeśvara's day.

Durgā is the renowned Indian goddess; in certain iconographic prayers, she is called *kāntārā,* of the wilderness. My guess is that in countless locations the pan-Indian name Durgā (Difficult-to-Approach) got laid over a tribal deity. Here her grotto is a rock crevasse or hollow, probably a local site, near where Yogeśvara studied the ceremony.

लेखामनङ्गपुरतोरणकान्तिभाजमिन्दोर्विलोकय तनूदरि नूतनस्य ।
देशान्तरप्रणयिनोरपि यत्र यूनोर्नूनं मिथः सखि मिलन्ति विलोकितानि ॥
[SR 903]

lekhāmanaṅgapuratoraṇakāntibhājamindor vilokaya tanūdari nūtanasya
deśāntarapraṇayinor api yatra yūnor nūnaṃ mithaḥ sakhi milanti vilokitāni

lekhām. faintly discernible streak of the new crescent moon
anaṅga. bodiless, incorporeal, phantom
pura. city
toraṇa. arch
kānti. lovely
bhājam. place, receptacle, desire
indoḥ. at the moon
vilokaya. (second-person imp.) look
tanūdari. (f.) (voc.) O slim-waisted woman
nūtanasya. young, fresh, new (adj. with moon)
deśāntara. (in a) far-off country, abroad
praṇayinoḥ. of two lovers
api. indeed
yatra. where
yūnoḥ. bound; a cord or connection (adj. with lovers)
nūnaṃ. surely, right now
mithaḥ. mutually, separately
sakhi. (voc.) friend
milanti. meet, come together
vilokitāni. the gazes

Slim-Waisted Friend

Slim-waisted friend,
look—
spreading its arch
over Love's
phantom city,
the faint crescent moon—
where the separate
gazes of lovers
parted to separate
countries meet.

Rājaśekhara, writing in the ninth and tenth centuries, shows up repeatedly (113 poems) in Vidyākara's *Subhāṣitaratnakoṣa.* Rājaśekhara composed a handbook of poetic training, the *Kāvyamimāṃsā,* giving detailed instruction on how poets might use language. The book also outlines how a poet maintains rigorous discipline: which hours of the day should be dedicated to study, writing, hygiene, and practice in the martial arts; and what hours should be set aside for lovemaking and sleep. All this presumes a carefully regulated domestic life. Nothing could be further from, say, Yogeśvara's penchant for travel in out-of-the-way locales or his searches for old ritual.

Wikipedia notes that "Rājaśekhara wrote the play [*Karpuramañjari*] to please his wife, Avantisundarī, a woman of taste and accomplishment. He is perhaps the only ancient Indian poet to acknowledge a woman for her contributions to his literary career."

The seven-word compound at the beginning of this poem refers to the *induḥ* (moon). *Anaṅga* means disembodied, incorporeal, and characterizes *pura* (city). The word is also an epithet for Kāma, lord of carnal desire.

यः कौमारहरः स एव हि वरस्ता एव चैत्रक्षपास्
ते चोन्मिलितमालतीसुरभयः प्रौढाः कदम्बानिलाः ।
सा चैवास्मि तथापि धैर्य सुरतव्यापारलीलाविधौ
रेवारोधसि वेतसीतरुतले चेतः समुत्कण्ठते ॥
[PE]

yaḥ kaumāraharaḥ sa eva hi varastā eva caitrakṣapās
te conmilitamālatīsurabhayaḥ prauḍhāḥ kadambānilāḥ
sā caivāsmi tathāpi dhairya suratavyāpāralīlāvidhau
revārodhasi vetasītarutale cetaḥ samutkaṇṭhate

yaḥ [and] *sa.* he who
kaumāra-haraḥ. virginity-taker
eva hi. surely, still indeed
varastā. (m.) lover
eva. also
caitra-kṣapāḥ. nights of Caitra, the spring month
te. these (are)
ca. and
unmilita-mālatī. blossomed-jasmine
surabhayaḥ. fragrances (with winds)
prauḍhāḥ. (we are) married, middle-aged
kadambā-nilāḥ. *kadamba*-tree winds
sā. she, the woman
ca. also
eva. surely, still
asmi. I am
tathā-api. thus, why, how is it
dhairya. unending
surata-vyāpāra. lovemaking-occupied
līlā-vidhau. game-traditions
revā-rodhasi. on the banks of Reva (Nārmadā) River
vetasī. cane, rushes, reeds
taru. groves
tale. ground, banks
cetaḥ. (my) heart
samutkaṇṭhate. mourns, pines (literally, lifts up the throat)

Nights of Jasmine and Thunder

Nights of jasmine and thunder,
torn petals,
wind in the tangled *kadamba* trees—
nothing has changed.
Spring comes again and we've
simply grown older.
In the cane groves of Nārmadā River
he deflowered my
girlhood before we were
married.
And I grieve for those faraway nights
we played at love
by the water.

An early glimpse into eco-poetics. The elements of nature, specific and familiar, conspire in the speaker's memory with the mood of love. Plants, wind, thunder, the seasons, the river. Lady Śīlābhaṭṭārikā eroticizes the bioregion or, from another perspective, ritualizes, sanctifies the landscape. Most Indians know the *kadamba* tree (*Neolamarckia cadamba*) as an emblem of Krishna. In Punjabi miniature paintings or the wall paintings of Mithila, the tree is an emblem of his presence.

There is a second version of the poem, very close in vocabulary and temper. Yet the two poems observe the geography from different perspectives.

यः कौमारहरः स एव च वरस्ताश्चन्द्रगर्भा निशाः
प्रोन्मीलन्नवमालतीसुरभयस्ते ते च विन्ध्यानिलाः ।
सा चैवास्मि तथापि धैर्यसुरतव्यापारलीलाभृतां
किं मे रोधसि वेतसीवनभुवां चेतः समुत्कण्ठते ॥

The Man Who First Took My Flower

The man who first
took my flower is
still with me.
The moon-drenched nights have returned.

Fresh jasmine blows in from
the Vindhya Range
and the girl is still me.
But her heart?
It grieves for those nights
we stole off to the riverbank
and made love in the
cane groves
forever.

Thinking this over ten years ago, I wrote something like the following.

According to one critic, the first version has a flaw. Poetry handbooks do not permit the *mālatī*, a jasmine, to bloom in Caitra, the lunar month March to April. If Śīlā got her botany wrong, the complaints would be a sound eco-criticism of her best poem.

Or is it possible that Śīlābhaṭṭārikā's poem, which was selected by Śarṅgadhara for his anthology five hundred years after she wrote it, became scrambled, misremembered, or rewritten along the way? Perhaps by someone not familiar with botanical detail? Śīlā certainly recalls the *mālatī* blooming—blooming the season she would make love all night on the riverbank as a girl. But having aged, has she confused the lunar month of Caitra with another?

Sanskrit's rich vocabulary is full of words with complex overtones. Several meanings may easily meet in a single term, so no word-by-word translation is likely to match the original. Dictionaries, for instance, give *mālatī* (jasmine) the additional meaning of "virgin." The scent of jasmine, the newly opened flower releasing its fragrance. The image also refers to the poet herself, those far-off nights of Caitra.

The second version is from Vidyākara's *Subhāṣitaratnakoṣa*. How could it be so much the same and yet so different? It invokes a different geographic feature. Was it meant to answer a criticism leveled at the first version? Could one have been a draft?

Having gone into the jasmine-scented darkness, into the dictionary, into the poet's rhythm—set in the meter known as *śārdūla-vikrīdita* (tiger's play)—to me, both poems seem necessary. Which would you discard? The moon-drenched nights (*candra-garba-niśā*), or the breeze scented with *kadamba* blossoms (*kadambā-nilāḥ*)? If you could have only one, which would it be: Vindhya Range or Nārmadā River?

ŚĪLĀBHAṬṬĀRIKĀ

दूती त्वं तरुणी युवा स चपलः श्यामस्तमोभिर्दिशः
संदेशस् सरहस्य एष विपिने संकेतकावासकः ।
भूयो भूय इमे वसन्तमरुतश्चेतो नयन्त्यन्यथा
गच्छ क्षेमसमागमाय निपुणं रक्षन्तु ते देवताः ॥
[SP 80]

dūtī tvaṃ taruṇī yuvā sa capalaḥ śyāmastamobhir diśaḥ
saṃdeśas sarahasya eṣa vipine saṃketakāvāsakaḥ
bhūyo bhūya ime vasantamarutaś ceto nayanty anyathā
gaccha kṣemasamāgamāya nipuṇaṃ rakṣantu te devatāḥ

dūtī. messenger-girl
tvaṃ. you (are)
taruṇī. slender, young
yuvā. (m.) youth
sa. he (is)
capalaḥ. inconstant, wandering
śyāmas. dark
tamobhir. (inst.) torpor, darkness (in this case, clouds)
diśaḥ. sky
saṃdeśas. message, dispatch
sarahasya. secret
eṣa. this man
vipine. in the forest
saṃketakāvāsakaḥ. (bv. cmpd. with *eṣa*)
saṃketaka. tryst, assignation
āvāsakaḥ. making love
bhūyo bhūya. blows, blows (of the wind)
ime. these
vasanta-marutaḥ. spring winds
ceto. heart
nayanti. they lead
anyathā. elsewhere, astray
gaccha. (second-person imp.) go
kṣema. quickly, easily
samāgamāya. to the meeting
nipuṇaṃ. craft, art
rakṣantu. may they protect
te. the
devatāḥ. gods, guardian deities

You, My Messenger

You, my messenger
are a tender sprig
but I trust you with a secret dispatch.
Go to the wind-tossed forest
where that dark man
awaits me.
Black clouds trouble the heavens,
spring breezes stir and the heart
also stirs.
But go to him safely.
May the gods keep a close
watch
over your art.

The winds blow the heart *anyathā* (elsewhere or astray). Still, the woman must send her *dūtī* (messenger) to set up the tryst, however much anxiety it causes her. She dispatches the girl with a blessing that her *nipuṇaṃ* (craft or skill) be supernaturally protected. The protectors invoked are the *devatā:* not the big gods (*deva*), but the local spirits who come out of the land, the ones who watch over this patch of forest, these fields, the nearby creeks or springs.

Waiting in the woods, the lover could be *śyāmaḥ* (dark), as the sky is dark (the adjective could go with both), reminding her of Krishna, whose straying is legendary and who bears the epithet *Śyāma* (Dark One). Certainly the unnamed lover is *capala* (inconstant or wandering), at the mercy of the winds that are *bhūyo bhūya* (blowing, blowing), continuously tossing this way and that.

किमपि किमपि मन्दं मन्दमासत्तियोगाद्
अविचलितकपोलं जल्पतोश्च क्रमेण ।
अशिथिलपरिरम्भव्यापृतैकैकदोष्णोर्
अविदितगतयामा रात्रिरेव व्यरंसीत् ॥
[SR 598]

kimapi kimapi mandaṃ mandam āsattiyogād
avicalitakapolaṃ jalpatoś ca krameṇa
aśithilaparirambhavyāpṛtaikaika doṣṇor
aviditagatayāmā rātrir eva vyaraṃsīt

kimapi kimapi. this thing, that thing
mandaṃ mandam. softly softly
āsatti. tight, fast
yogād. embrace
avicalita. intimate union, tightly together
kapolaṃ. cheek
jalpatoḥ. talking, whispering
ca. and
krameṇa. in the course of time
aśithila-parirambha-vyāpṛta-eka-eka-doṣṇoḥ. (bv. cmpd.) while the two (of us) were wrapped tightly in one another's arms, engaged in lovemaking
aśithila. tight, close
parirambha. embrace, lovemaking
vyāpṛta. engaged, occupied
eka eka. one-in-one
doṣṇoḥ. arms
avidita. not known
gata-yāmā. vanishing, fleeing
rātriḥ. night
eva. indeed
vyaraṃsīt. (root: *vi-ram*, to stop) came to an end

Through the Whole Night

Through the whole night we slowly
made love,
body pressed against body,
cheek against cheek.
We spoke every thought that came into mind.
Lost in each other's arms
lost in words, we never noticed
dawn had come
    the night flown.

This dawn song—or *alba* as troubadours of Provence called such songs—gives voice to the hour when daylight comes and the lovers must separate. Bhavabūti's poem opens with soft *m* sounds: *kimapi kimapi mandaṃ mandam. Kimapi* is an indefinite: something, anything, whatever. Doubling it gives the sense of everything, anything at all. *Mandaṃ mandam . . . jalpatoḥ:* us talking softly, softly.

The poem comes from the drama *Uttararāmacarita.* As with so many of the best poems, it appears in two variations, the slight difference being only grammatical, nothing to do with meaning. It has been called the finest poem in Sanskrit by a number of critics.

In *The Peacock's Egg,* Jeffrey Masson recounts a story. When Bhavabhūti had finished writing his play, he excitedly approached his colleague, the dramatist and poet Kālidāsa, who was absorbed in a chess game. Bhavabhūti read the whole play aloud. Kālidāsa never looked up from the chessboard. When the reading was finished, Kālidāsa lifted his hand, checkmated his opponent, turned to his playwright friend, and declared the drama perfect—except for one superfluous *m.* Bhavabhūti removed an *m* from this verse. It changed the second-to-last word from *evam* to *eva. Evam* means "thus," lending a rather heavy emphasis. The more understated *eva* is a filler word, a nearly unnoticeable tiny gesture—something that in our own poetry we might do with a line break.

"Poetry presents the thing in order to convey the feeling. It should be precise about the thing and reticent about the feeling," wrote Chinese poet Wei T'ai in the eleventh century. It is Bhavaḅhūti's reticence that lets the poem's feeling "linger as an aftertaste."

ये नाम केचिदिह नः प्रथयन्त्यवज्ञां जानन्ति ते किमपि तान्प्रति नैष यत्नः ।
उत्पत्स्यते तु मम कोऽपि समानधर्मा कालो ह्ययं निरवधिर्विपुला च पृथ्वी ॥
[SR 1731]

ye nāma kecidiha naḥ prathayanty avajñāṃ jānanti te kimapi tānprati naiṣa yatnaḥ
utpalsyate tu mama ko'pi samānadharmā kālo hyayaṃ niravadhir vipulā ca lakṣmī

ye. (they) who
nāma. good name, reputation
kecid. some people
iha. here, in the world
naḥ. of us (my)
prathayanti. (they) cause to spread about
avajñāṃ. contempt, disrespect
jānanti. (they) know
te. they
kimapi. something, anything
tānprati. for them
na. not
eṣa. this
yatnaḥ. work, performance (writing)

utpalsyate. will be born, will arise
tu. but
mama. of me
ko'pi. someone
samāna-dharmā. (bv. cmpd., *samāna-dharman*) (m.) one with the same character or faith, same-hearted
kālo. time
hi. because
ayaṃ. it, this
niravadhiḥ. endless, limitless
vipulā. extensive, wide, long
ca. and
lakṣmī. fortune

Critics Scoff

Critics scoff
at my work
and declare their contempt—
no doubt they've got
their own little wisdom.
I write nothing for them.
But because time is
endless and our planet
vast, I write these
poems for a person
who will one day be born
with my sort of heart.

"Criticism is for poets as ornithology is for the birds," wrote John Cage. Bhavabhūti has scant doubt that future generations will honor his work. The reader who will arise, *utpalsyate*, is somebody of the same faith, heart, or discipline, *samāna-dharmā*. The word *dharma*, a complex one in India's culture, is perhaps close to what North Americans mean by a spiritual path, a good road that one follows through life. See Dharmakīrti's "No One Visible" for another poet's sense of how hard the road is. In the *Subhāṣitaratnakoṣa,* the final word is *lakṣmī* (fortune), but Ingalls says to read *pṛthvī* (earth) "because time is endless and the earth wide."

अलमतिचपलत्वात्स्वप्नमायोपमत्वात्
परिणतिविरसत्वात्संगमेन प्रियायाः ।
इति यदि शतकृत्वस्तत्त्वमालोकयामस्
तदपि न हरिणाक्षीं विस्मरत्यन्तरात्मा ॥
[SR 477]

alam aticapalatvāt svapnamāyopamatvāt
pariṇativirasatvāt saṃgamena priyāyāḥ
iti yadi śatakṛtvas tattvam ālokayāmas
tad api na hariṇākṣīṃ vismaraty antarātmā

alam. enough, equal to
ati-capalatvāt. extremely brief, instantaneous
svapna. dream
māyā. illusion
upamatvāt. is like, resembles
pariṇati. consequence, natural end
virasatvāt. juiceless, insipid, leaving a bad taste
saṃgamena. sexual union
priyāyāḥ. (f.) with (your) lover
iti. thus
yadi. though
śata. one hundred
kṛtvaḥ. times
tattvam. this truth
ālokayāmas. I reflect, study, consider
tad-api. nonetheless
na. does not
hariṇa-akṣīṃ. (bv. cmpd.) (f.) antelope-eyed-one
vismarati. forget
antarātmā. (my) inner self, heart

A Snatch of Dream

A snatch of dream,
a juggler's contrivance—
making love to her
lasts hardly an instant,
then leaves a bad taste in the mouth.
A hundred times
I reflect on this "truth"
but still can't forget
the lady's antelope eyes.

In Vidyākara's eleventh-century anthology, nineteen poems carry Dharmakīrti's name. Nobody knows whether the Dharmakīrti who wrote them was the seventh-century Buddhist logician of the same name. The poems are certainly Buddhist in vocabulary and philosophy. This poem uses both *svapna* (dream) and *māyā* (illusion or contrivance)—words that recur in Buddhist *sūtras*. Both terms show up famously in a verse embedded in the *Diamond Sūtra:* "As a dream, an illusion . . . so should all compounded things be regarded." Likewise, what I've translated as "truth" is a technical Buddhist term: *tattva* (thus-ness).

Dharmakīrti's poems use twists of logic, deconstructions of grammar, and a trained metaphysical mind to expose the vulnerable heart. He shows himself unable to dwell in logic alone, and cannot abandon sexual love—though it ends up *vi-rasa-tvāt:* literally, juiceless; more colloquially, leaving a bad taste. No matter how decisively the Mahayana Buddhist *sūtras* and commentaries, as well as his own logical mind, insist that love is temporary, illusory, or in the end disappointing, a deeper instinct keeps driving Dharmakīrti back to his beloved. He calls her *hariṇa-akṣīṃ* (girl with antelope eyes). That feral quality of desire—a dash of animal wildness—before which logic stands powerless.

In Light of India, Octavio Paz's book on his six years in India, reflects on the mystery of Dharmakīrti's identity: "In Vidyākara's anthology there are various poems attributed to a Dharmakīrti. Reading this name, I rubbed my eyes: was it possible that the author of these erotic poems was also the severe Buddhist logician? Professor Ingalls [translator of the anthology into English] dispelled my doubts: the passionate, sensuous, and ironic poet and the closely reasoning and sharp-minded philosopher are almost certainly one and the same."

वहति न पुरः कश्चित्पश्चान्न कोऽप्यनुयाति मां
न च नवपदक्षुण्णो मार्गः कथं न्वहमेककः ।
भवतु विदितं पूर्वव्यूढोऽधुना खिलतां गतः
स खलु बहलो वामः पन्था मया स्फुटमुर्जितः ॥
[SR 1729]

vahati na puraḥ kaścit paścānna ko'py anuyāti māṃ
na ca navapadakṣuṇṇo mārgaḥ kathaṃ nvaham ekakaḥ
bhavatu viditaṃ pūrvavyūḍho'dhunā khilatāṃ gataḥ
sa khalu bahalo vāmaḥ panthā mayā sphuṭam urjitaḥ

vahati. goes
na. not
puraḥ. before, ahead
kaścit. anyone
paścāt. after, behind
na. not (no one)
ko'pi. someone
anuyāti. follows
māṃ. me
na. not
ca. and
nava-pada-kśuṇṇo. (bv. cmpd. with *mārga*) new-footprint-trod
mārgaḥ. road
kathaṃ. how
nu. now
aham. I (am)
ekakaḥ. alone, solitary
bhavatu. let it be
viditaṃ. known
pūrva-vyūḍho. of the old masters, men of meters (poets)
adhunā. now
khilatāṃ. deserted, barren, wasteland
gataḥ. the way
sa. the, it
khalu. indeed
bahalo. bushy, dense, thick, choked
vāmaḥ. pleasant, agreeable; also, wrong, left-handed
panthā. road, highway
mayā. by me
sphuṭam. clearly, evidently
urjitaḥ. abandoned

No One Visible

No one visible up ahead,
no one approaches
from behind.
No fresh footprint breaks the road.
Am I alone?
This much is clear—
the path the ancient
poets opened
is choked with brush,
and I've long since left
the public thoroughfare.

Nobody's said it better. Poetry is a solitary, bitter path. In art as in all spiritual pursuits, you travel alone. You cannot even follow the dead. Their way closed up behind them—it is *bahalo,* brush filled, thick, choked off. And the easy road—the road taken by groupies, devotees, followers, or fans—has a thousand sideshows but won't lead to the goal. Good art is what the solitary poet (or theater troupe, or orchestra) brings back to the community. The word *vāmaha,* which Dharmakīrti uses to characterize the common road, can mean broad and pleasant, or left-handed, deviant, crooked, misleading. Rarely has anyone put this double meaning to such use. The *pūrva-vyuḍha* are the old masters, the ancients. The term could refer to spiritual masters, but as this is a poem, I take it to mean poets. One definition the dictionary gives is "those who use meters," that is, writers of poetry.

FROM A POEM AT THE RIGHT MOMENT

Anonymous

दिने दिने गच्छति नाथ यौवनम्
यभस्व नित्यं यदि शक्तिरस्ति चेद् ।
मृतस्य को दास्यति पिण्डसन्निधौ
तिलोदकैः सार्धमलोमशं भगम् ।।
[PRM p109]

dine dine gacchati nātha yauvanam
yabhasva nityaṃ yadi śaktirasti ced
mṛtasya ko dāsyati piṇḍasannidhau
tilodakaiḥ sārdham alomaśaṃ bhagam

dine dine. (loc. abs.) day after day
gacchati. (loc. abs.) is going past
na. nor
atha. again (will there be)
yauvanam. youth
yabhasva. fuck (me) (second-person imp.)
nityaṃ. (indeclinable) now, by all means
yadi. if
śaktir. power, capability
asti. there is (for you)
ced. if
mṛtasya. in death
ko. who
dāsyati. will give
piṇḍa-sannidhau. rice ball (traditionally a corpse is cremated with a rice ball in its mouth)
tilodakaiḥ. with sesame seeds
sa-ardhaṃ. along with (literally, with the other half)
a-lomaśaṃ. hairless (shaved)
bhagam. (f.) sex organ

Day by Day Goes Past

Day by day goes past, and youth too.
Fuck me now
if you can—
Dead, who will give you
along with the
sesame-rice ball
a sweetly shaved
cunt?

This poem is inexcusably direct for Sanskrit. Official rules, for a tradition that valued suggestion or indirection over direct statement, forbade the use of sexually explicit words in poetry. The terms in question—*yabhasva* (fuck me), and *bhaga* ("the bestower" of pleasure, or of birth)—won't appear too raw if you look them up in a dictionary. To find them in a Sanskrit poem, though, would be more troubling than any words I could use to translate them. The poem is so outside the tradition of Indian poetry that it was probably never written down. The editors of *A Poem at the Right Moment* therefore transcribed the oral version.

पुराभूदस्माकं प्रथममविभिन्ना तनुरियं
ततोऽनु त्वं प्रेयानहमपि हताशा प्रियतमा ।
इदानीं नाथस्त्वं वयमपि कलत्रं किमपरं
मयाप्तं प्राणानां कुलिशकठिनानां फलमिदम् ॥
[SR 646, AM 81]

purābhūd asmākaṃ prathamam avibhinnā tanur iyaṃ
tato'nu tvaṃ preyān aham api hatāśā priyatamā
idānīṃ nāthastvaṃ vayam api kalatraṃ kimaparaṃ
mayāptaṃ prāṇānāṃ kuliśakaṭhinānāṃ phalam idam

purā. previously
abhūt. was
asmākaṃ. our, my
prathamam. at first
a-vi-bhinnā. never separated
tanuḥ. body
iyaṃ. this
tato. then
anu. surely
tvaṃ. you
preyān. the beloved
aham. I (was)
api. surely, also
hata-āśāḥ-priyatamā. (bv. cmpd.) ruined-hope-beloved, desolate mistress
idānīṃ. now, currently
nāthaḥ. the husband, lord
tvaṃ. you (are)
vayam. I (am)
api. in fact
kalatraṃ. the wife
kimaparaṃ. what else? what's next?
hatānāṃ. destroyed, struck, tragic
prāṇāṃ. life
kuliśa. of the thunderbolt's
kaṭhinānāṃ. cruelty, hardship
phalam. fruit, result, end
idam. this (is)

Those First Days

Those first days
of untempered love
my body and
your body were never apart.
The seasons turned.
You came to be my cherished lord,
I the desolate mistress.
Now you're the husband,
I'm the wife,
what will come when the year turns again?
Life must be cruel as a thunderbolt
if this is
where it ends.

Purā . . . tato . . . kimaparaṃ . . . The poem's weight gets carried by these little, nearly invisible words: "In the beginning . . . then . . . what next . . . ?" You can feel the cycle revolving inexorably. Poems such as this appear in anthologies that were divided into chapters; these conveyed the reader through love's cycles, from the awakening of desire to the desolation of love. Desolation might take the form of ripening pain, or the heartbreaking end of an affair.

Translation often has to reach for context and cultural material that may not be apparent in the original, but needs to be present as part of its underlying metabolism. Such material is implicit in the poem's ecosystem if not explicit in the words. See Vikaṭanitambā's "You Ignored" for the phrase *premnaḥ pariṇatim* (cycle or seasons of love). Readers of the great Sanskrit anthologies would see Bhāvadevī's poem in the context of these cycles. My translation's phrase "the seasons turned" is not "in" the original words; it pervades the anthologies, though.

Eliot Weinberger speaks to this when he writes of translation, "Effects that cannot be reproduced in the corresponding line can usually be picked up elsewhere . . . which is why it is more difficult to translate a single poem than a book of poems." Weinberger also points out that for a translator, everything depends on the little words. (William Blake says, "Labour well the Minute Particulars, attend to the Little Ones.") Anybody can translate nouns. In Bhāvadevī's poem it is those little words, *first, then, what next,* that make you feel time hardening until love becomes *kaṭhina* (brittle).

कान्ते तल्पमुपागते विगलिता नीवी स्वयं बन्धनाद्
वासश्च श्लथमेखलागुणधृतं किञ्चिन्नितम्बे स्थितम् ।
एतावत् सखि वेद्मि केवलमहो तस्यांगसंगे पुनः
कोऽसौ काऽस्मि रत च किं सखि शपे स्वल्पापि मे न स्मृतिः ॥
[SP 137, SR 572]

kānte talpam upāgate vigalitā nīvī svayaṃ bandhanād
vāsaś ca ślathamekhalāguṇadhṛtaṃ kiṃcin nitambe sthitam
etāvat sakhi vedmi kevalam aho tasyāṅgasaṅge punaḥ
ko'sau kā'smi rata ca kiṃ sakhi śape svalpāpi me na smṛtiḥ

kānte. (my) lover
talpam. to bed
upāgate. when he came
vigalitā. untied
nīvī. skirt, sash
svayaṃ. by itself
bandhanāt. from the knot
vāsaḥ. dress
ca. and
ślatha-mekhalā-guṇa-dhṛtaṃ. (bv. cmpd. with dress) held by a loose girdle cord
kiṃcit. somehow
nitambe. on (my) hip
sthitam. stayed
etāvat. this
sakhi. dear friend
vedmi. I know
kevalam. only
aho. indeed
tasyāṅga-saṅge. when his arms wrapped (me)
punaḥ. again
ko'sau. who is he
kā'smi. who am I
rata. in sexual union
ca. and
kiṃ. what
sakhi. dear friend
śape. I swear
svalpa-api. even a little
me. by me
na. is not
smṛtiḥ. remembered

My Lover

My lover
stepped towards the bed.
Somehow the skirt
clung to my hips
but the knot came undone by itself.
What can I say?
Nothing makes sense in his arms
not who I am
not who is taking me.
Is it me that comes?
Is it him?

Ko'sau kā'smi rata ca kiṃ: Who is he, who am I, what is this sexual pleasure? There is no good parallel in English for *rata,* which in Sanskrit sounds delicate, cherished, meaning both the act of intercourse and the fever and ecstasy that accompany it. Most of our English terms sound too raw or too clinical. A feminine version of the Sanskrit noun *ratī* is personified as a consort of Kāma, the love god.

Attributed in the anthologies to a woman poet, Vikaṭanitambā, the poem also shows up in the *Amaruśataka.* More evidence that the Amaru collection is an early anthology, not the work of a single author.

Known for her clean, unpretentious style, avoiding the forced figures of speech used too frequently by poets, Vikaṭanitambā lived no later than the early ninth century. One of her extant poems depicts her husband as coarse, illiterate, struggling painfully with Sanskrit pronunciation. If this was the case, she could have had—one critic suggests it—an unhappy marriage. A later poet notes that she was widowed, then remarried. Only six poems of hers survive.

अनालोच्य प्रेम्णः परिणतिमनादृत्य सुहृद-
स्त्वयाऽकाण्डे मानः किमिति सरले प्रेयसि कृतः ।
समाकृष्टा ह्येते विरहदहनोद्भासुरशिखाः
स्वहस्तेनांगारास्तदलमधुनाऽरण्यरुदितैः ॥
[SP 134]

analocya premṇaḥ pariṇatim anādṛtya suhṛdas
tvayā'kāṇḍe mānaḥ kimiti sarale preyasi kṛtaḥ
samākṛṣṭā hyete virahadahanodbhāsuraśikhāḥ
svahastenāṃgārās tad alam adhunā'raṇyaruditaiḥ

anālocya. ignoring, disregarding
premṇaḥ. love
pariṇatim. cycles, transformations, maturing
anādṛtya. without respecting
suhṛdaḥ. friends
tvayā. by you
akāṇḍe. without cause
mānaḥ. coldness, jealous accusation
kim-iti. why
sarale-preyasi. (loc.) (at your) true, sincere lover
kṛtaḥ. is made (with *mānaḥ*)
samākṛṣṭā. gathered, drawn to oneself
hi. (excl.) surely
ete. these
viraha-dahana-udbhāsura-śikhāḥ. (bv. cmpd.) flaring with the angry fire of betrayal
viraha. separation, betrayal
dahana. burning
udbhāsura. glow
śikhāḥ. flames
sva-hastena. by your own hand
aṃgārās. coals
tad-alam. enough of this
adhunā. now
araṇya-ruditaiḥ. forest-weeping, wild lament, animal howls

You Ignored

You ignored
the turning seasons of love,
shook off advice
and treated your lover with
cold disregard.
Bright
coals of betrayal
gathered to your own bare breasts,
yet you cry out in rage
like a wild
animal wounded.

These opening words, to my mind, capture the entire tradition of love as the Sanskrit poets conceived of it. That is, love follows its own seasons or cycles. The *pariṇatim* are the cycles, transformations, ripening of *premṇaḥ* (love). I read the classic anthologies or collections as almanacs: they provide chapters on each of the natural seasons (India knew six: spring, summer, rainy season, autumn, winter, late winter) as well as the seasons of eros, which revolve by their own natural laws. To ignore the changes, to willfully neglect them, was to ensure anguish. The coals in the poem get gathered, drawn together, by *sva-hastena* (your own hands). *Araṇya-ruḍita* are forest-cries: wilderness or animal howls.

कृष्णेनाम्भो गतेन रन्तुमधुना मृद् भक्षिता स्वेच्छया
सत्यं कृष्ण क एवमाह मुसली मिथ्याम्भ पश्याननम् ।
व्यादेहीति विकासिते ऽथ वदने दृष्ट्वा समस्तम् जगत्
माता यस्य जगाम विस्मयपदम् पायात् स वः केशवः ॥
[PE 18]

kṛṣṇenāmbho gatena rantum adhunā mṛd bhakṣitā svecchayā
satyaṃ kṛṣṇa ka evam āha musalī mithyāmbha paśyānanam
vyādehīti vikāsite 'tha vadane dṛṣṭvā samastaṃ jagat
mātā yasya jagāma vismayapadam pāyāt sa vaḥ keśavaḥ

kṛṣṇeṇa. by Krishna
ambho. mother
gatena. went
rantum. to play
adhunā. now
mṛd. (f.) dirt
bhakṣitā. was eaten
sva-icchayā. (ind.) at his desire
satyaṃ. true
ka. who
evam. thus
āha. said
musalī. "the one with a club," Krishna's brother Balarama
mithyā. (ind.) wrong, a lie
ambha. mother
paśya. (imp.) look
ananam. (at my) mouth
vi-ādehi. (*vy-ā-dā*) (imp.) open your mouth
iti. [quotation marks]
vikāsite. (loc. abs.) when he opened his mouth
atha. now
vadane. into his mouth
dṛṣṭvā. having looked
samastaṃ. entire
jagat. world (universe)
mātā. Mother
yasya. of him
jagāma. went
vismaya-padam: to the foot of wonder
vismaya. to wonderment, astonishment
padam. foot
pāyāt. (optative) may he protect
sa. he
vaḥ. you (all)
keśavaḥ. epithet of Krishna

Krishna Went Out to Play

Krishna went out to play, Mother
and ate dirt
Is that true, Krishna?
Who said it?
Your brother
A lie! Look in my mouth—
Open it—
and awestruck she saw the
whole Universe
May Keśava protect you.

A poem based on one of the well-known tales of Krishna's childhood. Sanskrit scholar Jeffrey Masson writes, "the emphasis is on the elusiveness of the epiphany." Caṇḍaka's poem shows Krishna "as a young boy, impetuous, playful, disdainful of his elders, who at a given moment allows them an insight into his mystery." No matter how often Krishna exposes his identity by accomplishing superhuman feats as an infant, everybody, including his foster mother, forgets that he is lord of the universe. Between his supernatural adventures, he behaves like a mischievous child, and this is central to his *līlā* (divine play). Vaiṣṇava philosophers explain it all theologically. Caṇḍaka's audience would have known the story intimately from hearing it during their own childhoods.

Krishna is an avatar, descended to Earth to slay a serpent demon that has been terrorizing the region. His mother is really a foster mother who found him in rushes by the river. Psychoanalytic-minded Western scholars make a great deal of the theme: forgetting, remembering, forgetting again. The play between vulnerable infant and impossibly powerful hero draws attention, along with the motif of humble foster parents: "the myth of the birth of the hero." The charm of Caṇḍaka's poem is that it compresses the familiar into a tight lyric—a magical talisman you could slip in your pocket. The quick exchange between Krishna and his mother occurs without *iti* (quotation marks) until after *paśyānanam* (look in my mouth!). In Sanskrit, quotations are indicated by *iti*, and typically occur at the end of quoted text. Generally there is no marker to show where quotation begins, adding to the potential for ambiguity.

Blessings at verse-end are common to religious prayers. Classical poets would insert them, sometimes ironically, sometimes for humor, though here I think the blessing is to seal the poem, the amulet, the way a craftsman would bless a nearly finished sculpture with a prayer that awakens the deity lying dormant within the *rūpa* (image).

Keśava (pronounced KAY-sha-va) is an epithet for Krishna that refers to his long hair.

दुर्दिननिशिथपवने निःसंचारासु नगरवीथिषु ।
पत्यौ विदेशयाते परं सुखं जघनचपलायाः ॥
[SR 825]

durdinaniśīthapavane niḥsaṃcārāsu nagaravīthiṣu
patyau videśayāte paraṃ sukhaṃ jaghanacapalāyāḥ

durdina. rainy day, bad weather
niśītha. night
pavane. (loc. abs. when [there are] night winds and rainy weather) wind
niḥsaṃcārāsu. deserted, empty of walkers (with streets)
nagara. city
vīthiṣu. (loc. abs.) (f.) streets, market
patyau. (loc. abs. when my husband) husband
videśa. abroad, another land
yāte. (loc. abs.) has gone
paraṃ. supreme, great
sukhaṃ. pleasure, delight, happily
jaghana-capalā. (bv. cmpd.) woman who moves (shakes) her hips; sexually exuberant
jaghana. hips, buttocks, loins, vulva
capalā. (f.) moving about, quavering, inconstant

Rainy Nights

Rainy nights
the city streets deserted
husband traveling
in a far-off land.
This is when Jaghanacapalā rejoices
she likes to sleep
around.

The key to this poem is a compound word, *jaghanacapalā,* which means a shaking of the hips or loins (or buttocks or vulva). The way it appears here, with a feminine ending, makes it a *bahuvṛhi* compound: woman who rocks her loins. Colloquially, this means something like "who sleeps around" or, more playfully, who shakes her tail feathers. But there is more. The poem shows up in an anthology attributed to a woman identified as Jaghanacapalā. This means that any reading since at least the twelfth century—the date of the anthology in which the poem appears—has taken it for a proper name as well as a woman's description. Hence it carries two meanings, and you need to translate both to get the force, the *śakti,* of the verse.

There's a further twist. *Jaghanacapalā* is also the name of a poetic meter or rhythm in Sanskrit, the two-line pattern this poem occurs in. Sanskrit metrical patterns carry vivid names, which must originate in dance. Others are *śārdūla-vikrīḍita* (tiger's play), Girl with a Ball, and so forth. The first handbook of India's art, the *Natyaśāstra* of Bharata Muni, traces the origins of art to a sacred theater—founded as a "Fifth Veda" by Brahma the Creator—that included dance, music, poetry, costume, and stagecraft. (A good translation of this origin myth appears in Daumal p. 43.) In the surviving dramas of Sanskrit, of which there are a great many, at moments of poignant or intense emotion, an actor breaks into dance, accompanied by music and the ceremonial recitation of a poem. Jaghanacapalā as a metrical pattern would have begun with the dance of a dramatic character and a poem that perhaps regulated her footwork.

The classical poets saw this as a particular skill, not easy to accomplish: working into a poem the name of its meter. This seems quite postmodern—like the painter Jasper Johns affixing to his canvas one of his rulers; or using a Savarin coffee can filled with paintbrushes for his *Painted Bronze* sculpture.

यदि कथंचित्प्राप्स्यामि प्रियं अकृतं कौतुकं करिष्यामि ।
पानीयं नवके शरावे यथा सर्वाङ्गेण प्रवेक्ष्यामि ।।
[HG 396.4]

yadi kathaṃcit prāpsyāmi priyaṃ akṛtaṃ kautukaṃ kariṣyāmi
pānīyaṃ navake śarāve yathā sarvāṅgeṇa pravekṣyāmi

yadi. if
kathaṃcit. somehow
prāpsyāmi. I should meet
priyaṃ. (my) lover
akṛtaṃ. undone, never-before-done
kautukaṃ. singular or surprising thing, a pleasure
kariṣyāmi. I will do, perform
pānīyaṃ. water
navake. newly made, new
śarāve. pot, clay jug, earthenware
yathā. as
sarva. all, complete
aṅgeṇa. with (my) body
pravekṣyāmi. I will enter

If He and I

If he and I
meet again
I'll give him something no
girl ever has,
whole
body coming and
going inside him
water in an earthenware
jar

Hemacandra (1088–1172) was a Jain scholar from what is now Gujarat State. Among the many topics he wrote on, including military policy and a prohibition on the use of weapons of mass destruction—such as crushing opponents with avalanches—was grammar. In his book some fine poems survive that don't appear anywhere else. This one is from a chapter on loan words into Sanskrit. It is the earthen jar, *śarāva,* that interests him—a touch of indigenous culture. It offers a twist on the image of the clay jug: newly worked earthenware needs to be seasoned with water before it will hold.

All three verbs *(prāpsyāmi, kariṣyāmi, pravekṣyāmi)* are future tense.

मेघैर्मेदुरमम्बरं वनभुवः श्यामास्तमालद्रुमैर्
　　नक्तं भीरुरयं त्वमेव तदिमं राधे गृहं प्रापय ।
इत्थं नन्दनिदेशितश्चलितयोः प्रत्यध्वकुञ्जद्रुमं
　　राधामाधवयोर्जयन्ति यमुनाकूले रहःकेलयः ॥

[GG 1.1]

meghair meduram ambaraṃ vanabhuvaḥ śyāmāstamāladrumair
　　naktaṃ bhīrur ayaṃ tvam eva tad imaṃ radhe gṛhaṃ prāpaya
itthaṃ nandanideśitaś calitayoḥ pratyadhva kuñjadrumaṃ
　　rādhāmādhavayor jayanti yamunākūle rahaḥ kelayaḥ

meghaiḥ. with clouds
meduram. darkened
ambaraṃ. sky
vanabhuvaḥ. forest groves
śyāmās. dark
tamāla. an evergreen
drumaiḥ. trees
naktaṃ. night
bhiruḥ. scared
ayaṃ. he
tvam. you
eva. indeed
tad. that
imaṃ. him
radhe. (voc.) O Radha
gṛhaṃ. home
prāpaya. take
itthaṃ. thus
nanda. Krishna's foster father
nideśitaḥ. directive
calitayoḥ. wandering (Krishna and Radha)
pratyadhva. past
kuñja. groves
drumaṃ. tree
rādhā. Radha, cowherd girl, beloved of Krishna
mādhava. Krishna
jayanti. conquer, overcome
yamunā. the Yamunā (Jumna) River
kūle. on the shore
rahaḥ. secret
kelayaḥ. desires, passions

Clouds Thicken the Sky

"Clouds thicken the sky,
the forests are
dark with tamāla trees.
He is afraid of night, Radha,
take him home."
They depart at Nanda's directive
passing on the way
thickets of trees.
But reaching Yamunā River, secret desires
overtake Radha and Krishna.

These final dozen lyrics come from what is considered the last great poem in the Sanskrit tradition, Jayadeva's twelth-century *Gīta-Govinda*. The title means song (*gīta*) of Krishna. Govinda is one of the common epithets or affectionate names for Krishna, and refers to his upbringing among cowherds. However, poets and singers can use it without reference to the tales of Krishna's childhood in a small riverside village of cowherds.

If my intuition is correct—that the origin of Sanskrit's incessant cloud-and-rain imagery lies in evocations of the spirits of nature—then Jayadeva begins with elements picked up from archaic shamanism or animist traditions. This stanza has received a huge amount of attention, almost since Jayadeva's own era, because of its ambiguity. Who is the speaker? *Nanda-nideśita* may mean that the opening, quoted voice (*īttham̩* is an alternate for *iti*, quotation marks) is the "directive" of Nanda, Krishna's foster father. But it could also mean the "joyous directive," a reasonable statement for a poem meant to lead to salvation. But that leaves obscure who the speaker might be. Why would Krishna, no longer a child, be afraid of the night? (He himself is the Dark One.) If the boy is frightened or the forest perilous, why would his father ask a cowherd girl of the same age to take the boy home through the dark, as though she would be untouched by fear? Whose home should she lead him to: her own or his? Or does *gr̥ham̩* (home), have an allegorical meaning? Jayadeva's poem never shows Krishna returning to the cottage of his foster parents.

On the banks of the Jumna River (*yamunākūle*), in a thicket of the white-blossoming dark-barked evergreens called *tamāla* (*Cinnamomum tamala*), the two young people are overpowered by *rahaḥ-kelayaḥ* (secret desires or passions). This sets the tone for what will follow: darkness, secrecy, anxiety; a fragrant springtime waking of passion; a mysterious, edgy uncertainty.

वाग्देवताचरितचित्रितचित्तसद्मा
    पद्मावतीचरणचारणचक्रवर्ती ।
श्रीवासुदेवरतिकेलिकथासमेतम्
    एतं करोति जयदेवकविः प्रबन्धम् ।।

[GG 1.2]

vāgdevatācaritacitritacittasadmā
    padmāvatīcaraṇacāraṇacakravartī
śrīvāsudevaratikelikathāsametam
    etaṃ karoti jayadevakaviḥ prabandham

vāk. Goddess of Speech
devatā. goddess
carita. rhythms
citrita. various
citta. heart
sadmā. dwelling in
padmāvatī. Jayadeva's wife
caraṇa. feet
cāraṇa. pilgrim, wanderer
cakravartī. "wheel-turner," king, chief, ruler
śrī. Lakṣmī, or the consort of Krishna, in this case Radha
vāsudeva. Krishna
rati. love making
keli. passion
kathā. story, legend
sametam. comprised of, constituted
etaṃ. this (with *prabhandam*)
karoti. (he) made
jayadeva-kavi. Jayadeva the poet
prabhandam. work of literature, poem in a variety of forms or meters; cantos

Jayadeva, Chief Poet on Pilgrimage

Jayadeva, chief poet on pilgrimage
to Padmavati's feet—
every craft of
Goddess Language
stored in his heart—
has assembled tales from the erotic encounters
of Krishna and Śri
to compose these cantos.

This, the poem's second verse, isolates the opening stanza as a momentary episode, background for what will follow, much as contemporary movies use an opening scene to set the tone. Credits then appear, naming the actors, director, producer, before setting the audience back into the opening scene but at a later time.

Jayadeva introduces his own name here, an occasional practice in Sanskrit poetry. In Northern India's *bhakti* songs, this signature line is called a *bhaṇita*. But the stanza serves also as invocation, a traditional benediction to remove obstacles. It gives praise to Vāg-Devī or Vāk, an old Indo-Aryan goddess of voice, poetry, and song. In the Vedas, Vāk appears at times as the primal force of the universe. Later in history (post-Vedic), she merges with a river goddess, Sarasvatī. For himself, Jayadeva uses the term *cakravartin* ("wheel-turner"). It means chief poet in this context, but is not a title to assume lightly. "Wheel-turner" refers to a great king whose ritual acts set the universe in motion. Early Buddhists picked up the word, using it as a title for Śākyamuni Buddha, who "turned (set in motion) the wheel" of Dharma.

Prabandha, what Jayadeva calls his poem, refers to a "composition" that includes chapters or cantos; it also suggests a binding of diverse styles, meters, and topics. Jayadeva says he has built it out of *kathā*. The word simply means "how" or "how did it happen"; as a noun, it means tale, story, or legend. The answer to how, of course, is *tathā* (just so—which is what Rudyard Kipling titled his book of origin tales). That Jayadeva assembles his poem from *kathās* says he drew on accounts already in circulation. Various parts of the full story must have been circulating through the countryside. His skill was to weave them into an erotic-devotional poem of high art—*kāvya*—and set it to music.

विहरति वने राधा साधारणप्रणये हरौ
विगलितनिजोत्कर्षादीर्ष्यावशेन गतान्यतः ।
क्वचिदपि लताकुञ्जे गुञ्जन्मधुव्रतमण्डली-
मुखरशिखरे लीना दीनाप्युवाच रहः सखीम् ॥

[GG 2.1]

viharati vane rādhā sādhāraṇapraṇaye harau
vigalitanijotkarṣād īrṣyāvaśena gatānyataḥ
kvacid api latākuñje guñjanmadhuvratamaṇḍalī-
mukharaśikhare līnā dīnāpy uvāca rahaḥ sakhīm

viharati. (loc. abs.) while wandering
vane. in the forest
rādhā. Radha
sādhāraṇa. around, everywhere
praṇaye. showing or making love
harau. (loc. abs.) Hari or Krishna
vigalita. loosened
nija-utkarṣāt. her hold (on him)
īrṣya-āvaśena. overcome with envy
gata-anyataḥ. went elsewhere
kvacid. wherever
api. indeed
latākuñje. in the vine-grove
guñjan. humming, buzzing
madhu-vrata. honeybees
maṇḍalī. circling
mukhara. noisily
śikhare. above, overhead
līnā. (adj. with Radha) absorbed
dīnā. miserable, wretched
api. surely
uvāca. she spoke, confided
rahaḥ. the secret
sakhīm. to (her) friend

Krishna Roamed the Forest

Krishna roamed the forest
taking the cowherdesses one after
another for love.
Radha's hold slackened,
jealousy drove her far off.
But over each refuge
in the vine-draped thickets
swarmed a loud circle of bees.
Miserable
she confided the secret
to her friend—

The *Gīta-Govinda* contains twenty-four songs, each set in three-line stanzas, meant by Jayadeva to be sung, as well as danced by his wife, Padmāvatī. The model evidently came from folk traditions. Binding the songs into a single story are narrative poems, composed not as song but in *kāvya* (art-poetry style). Great leaps in the narrative—blanks or gaps—allow for shifts in scene and the altered perspective of principal characters. Barbara Miller, the heroic scholar who dedicated years of travel and research to compiling the best edition of the *Gīta-Govinda*, points out that the principal point of view throughout is Radha's. In metaphysical terms, one would say the point of view is the human spirit's.

Notice how the natural orders—a *kuñja* (thicket) draped in vines; noisy honey gatherers—conspire in Radha's condition, *līnā dīnā* (absorbed, miserable). The *rahaḥ* (secret) she confides to her friend echoes the *rahaḥ* of the first verse, the secret desires that overcame her and Krishna in a different thicket. The vocabulary of this verse restores that first night of lovemaking to her, and to the reader. Bits of echoing vocabulary underscore what's been lost. A landscape of words torments Radha.

गणयति गुणग्रामं भामं भ्रमादपि नेहते
    वहति च परीतोषं दोषं विमुञ्चति दूरतः ।
युवतिषु बलस्तृष्णे कृष्णे विहारिणि मां विना
    पुनरपि मनो वामं कामं करोति करोमि किम् ॥
[GG 2.10]

gaṇayati guṇagrāmaṃ bhāmaṃ bhramād api nehate
    vahati ca parītoṣaṃ doṣaṃ vimuñcati dūrataḥ
yuvatiṣu balastṛṣṇe kṛṣṇe vihāriṇi māṃ vinā
    punar api mano vāmaṃ kāmaṃ karoti karomi kim

gaṇayati. (my heart) values
guṇagrāmaṃ. (his) collection of virtues
bhāmaṃ. wrath
bhramāt. due to his straying, infidelity
api. even
na-īhate. won't consider
vahati. pardons, forgives
ca. and
parītoṣaṃ. gladly
doṣaṃ. (his) faults, transgressions
vimuñcati. releases, denies
dūrataḥ. (when he is) far off
yuvatiṣu-balas-tṛṣṇe. (loc. abs.) craving for young women
kṛṣṇe. Krishna
vihāriṇi. when he wanders
māṃ. me
vinā. without
punaḥ. again
api. in fact
mano. my heart
vāmaṃ kāmaṃ. crooked or crazy desire
karoti. makes, conceives
karomi kim. what can I do?

Radha speaks

My conflicted heart
treasures even his infidelities.
Won't admit anger.
Forgives the deceptions.
Secret desires arise in my breasts.
What can I do? Krishna
hungry for lovers
slips off without me.
This torn heart grows only
more ardent.

Radha's heart makes or conceives *vāmaṃ kāmaṃ* (crooked desires). Is it because her heart pardons Krishna's faults and rejects anger? Or has something unexpectedly crooked, some crazy desire, awakened within her? Except for the final cry—*karomi kim* (what can I do?)—the subject of the entire verse is her *manas* (heart).

तानि स्पर्शसुखानि ते च तरलाः स्निग्धा दशोर्विभ्रमास्
        तद्वक्त्राम्बुजसौरभं स च सुधास्यन्दी गिरां वक्रिमा ।
सा बिम्बाधरमाधुरीति विषयासंगेऽपि चेन्मानसं
        तस्यां लग्नसमाधि हन्त विरहव्याधिः कथं वर्धते ॥

[GG 3.14]

tāni sparśasukhāni te ca taralāḥ snigdhā daśor vibhramās
        tad vaktrāmbujasaurabhaṃ sa ca sudhāsyandī girāṃ vakrimā
sā bimbādharamādhurīti viṣayāsaṃge'pi cen mānasaṃ
        tasyāṃ lagnasamādhi hanta virahavyādhiḥ kathaṃ vardhate

tāni. those
sparśa. of touch
sukhāni. delights
te. those
ca. and
taralāḥ. tremblings
snigdhā. enchanted
daśoḥ. of the eyes
vibhramāḥ. amorous, restless motions
tad-vaktra. from her mouth
ambuja. lotus
saurabhaṃ. fragrance
sa. the
ca. and
sudhā-syandī. nectar-flow
girāṃ. of words
vakrimā. ambiguous, forbidden
sā. the
bimba-ādhara. fruit-lip, nether lip
mādhuri. sweetness, honey
iti. thus
viṣaya. sense-pleasure
asaṅge. loose, untethered
api-cet. somehow
mānasaṃ. madly, passionately
tasyāṃ. on her
lagna-samādhi. fixed in meditation
hanta. (excl.)
viraha. of separation
vyādhiḥ. the disease, wound, torment
kathaṃ. how
vardhate. (does it) erupt, spring forth

Krishna Speaks

Krishna speaks

Every touch brought a new thrill.
Her eyes darted wildly.
From her mouth the
fragrance of lotus,
a rush of sweet forbidden words.
A droplet of juice
on her crimson lower lip.
My mind fixes these absent
sensations in a *samādhi*—
How is it that parted from her
the oldest
wound breaks open?

Krishna remembers a nectar-flow of words that were *vakrimā* (forbidden or ambiguous; literally, crooked, left-handed). Other words in his speech stand out. The first is *samādhi*, identified primarily with yoga. Both a meditation technique of fixing on or uniting with an object, and the condition of entering a spiritual trance, it sometimes suggests enlightenment. The Buddhists used the term, specifying precise states of trance.

Another term is *viraha* (separation)—one of two phases of *śṛṅgāra-rasa* (erotic love). The complementary phase is *sambhoga* (devouring or enjoying). The *vyādhi* (wound, dis-ease, or torment) cannot be assuaged by meditation. In fact the *samādhi* seems to reopen the old injury. The theology for an erotic mysticism could lie in this verse: Krishna himself reveals that yoga or religious practice won't keep the wound from suppurating.

Various mystical sects of Eastern India, their practices referred to as *sahaja*, believe erotic love must be incorporated into their rituals. For accounts of the sects see Edward Dimock Jr.'s book *The Place of the Hidden Moon* or Shashibhusan Dasgupta's *Obscure Religious Cults*. In particular, the Bauls of Bengal—wandering singers—openly mock the "dry path" of asceticism, and insist on a *rasika* (juicy) path.

आवासो विपिनायते प्रियसखीमालापि जालायते
तापोऽपि श्वसितेन दावदहनज्वालाकलापायते ।
सापि त्वद्विरहेण हन्त हरिणीरूपायते हा कथं
कन्दर्पोऽपि यमायते विरचयञ्शार्दूलविक्रीडितम् ।।

[GG 4.10]

āvāso vipināyate priyasakhīmālāpi jālāyate
tāpo'pi śvasitena dāvadahanajvālākalāpāyate
sāpi tvadvirahena hanta harinī rupāyate hā katham
kandarpo'pi yamāyate viracayañ śārdūlavikrīḍitam

āvāso. house
vipināyate. becomes a jungle
priya-sakhī. dear-friends
mālā. necklace
api. indeed
jālāyate. becomes a snare
tāpo. fever, passion (also, ascetic practice)
'pi. also
śvasitena. by breath
dāva-dahana-jvālā-kalāpāyate. turns into a searing, raging fire
sā. she
api. also
tvad-virahena. due to your absence
hanta. (voc.) O lover
harinī-rupāyate. (she) takes shape as a doe
hā. [cry of grief]
katham. how (is it that)?
kandarpo. love, sexual passion
'pi. (emph.)
yamāyate. becomes death (Yama)
viracayan. taking on (as a costume or mask), wearing
śārdūla-vikrīḍitam. tiger's play (also, name of a much-used metrical pattern)

Radha's messenger speaks

Her house has become
a pulsating jungle.
Her circle of girlfriends
a tightening snare.
Each time she breathes
a sheet of flame
bursts above the trees.
Krishna, you have gone—
in your absence she takes shape
as a doe crying out—
while Love turns to Death
and closes in
on tiger paws.

This is one of the stanzas into which Jayadeva weaves the Sanskrit name of the metrical pattern he is using: *śārdūla-vikrīḍita* (tiger's play). The last phrase of the verse literally reads: "love becomes death, taking on (wearing) the play of the tiger."

The entire verse is built on a special use of the verb form called *nāma-dhātu* (noun-verb). In this case, it is the transformation of one noun into another by making the second a verb—a nice touch in which everything transforms under the heat of Radha's anguish. The house "jungles," the circle of friends "snares," Radha "doe-shapes." Finally, love "deaths." *Kandarpa*, the word Jayadeva uses here for love—love personified, or sexual passion—is of "doubtful" etymology (Monier-Williams). An early meaning the grammarians give is "phallus."

अङ्गेष्वाभरणं करोति बहुशः पत्रेऽपि संचारिणि
प्राप्तं त्वां परिशङ्कते वितनुते शय्यां चिरं ध्यायति ।
इत्याकल्पविकल्पतल्परचनासंकल्पलीलाशत-
व्यासक्तापि विना त्वया वरतनुर्नैषा निशां नेष्यति ।।
[GG 6.11]

aṅgeṣv ābharaṇaṃ karoti bahuśaḥ patre'pi saṃcāriṇi
prāptaṃ tvāṃ pariśaṅkate vitanute śayyāṃ ciraṃ dhyāyati
ity ākalpavikalpatalparacanāsaṃkalpalīlāśata-
vyāsaktāpi vinā tvayā varatanur naiṣā niśāṃ neṣyati

aṅgeṣu. on her limbs
ābharaṇaṃ. adornment
karoti. she makes
bahuśaḥ. repeatedly
patra. a leaf
api. when even
saṃcāriṇi. quivers, moves about
prāptaṃ. have arrived
tvāṃ. you
pariśaṅkate. she imagines, fancies
vitanute. she spreads out
śayyāṃ. bed
ciraṃ. for a long time
dhyāyati. she studies, meditates
iti-ākalpa-vikalpa-talpa-racanā-saṃkalpa-līlā-śata-vyāsaktā. (bv. cmpd.) engaged in fantasies of one hundred varieties of love on the prepared bed
iti. thus
ākalpa. ornament
vikalpa. variety, art, fantasy
talpa. bed, couch
racanā. making
saṃkalpa. idea, conception, notion
līlā. play
śata. one hundred
vyāsaktā. engaged in
api. but
vinā. without
tvayā. you
varatanuḥ. the thin girl
na-eṣā [and] *neṣyati.* will she not (perish)
niśāṃ. tonight
neṣyati. will perish

She Ornaments Her Limbs

She ornaments her limbs
if a single leaf stirs
in the forest.
She thinks it's you, folds back
the bedclothes and stares
in rapture for hours.
Her heart conceives a hundred
amorous games on the well-prepared bed.
But without you this
wisp of a girl
will fade
to nothing tonight.

Internal rhyme and repetition of sound underlie each of *Gīta-Govinda*'s verses. Jayadeva particularly used *anuprāsa* (alliteration) and assonance, creating a trance-like quality in many of his stanzas. Barbara Miller writes of the poem: "alliterative combinations of consonants and vowels reinforce the meters and the sensuous imagery of the songs." This verse, written in classical *kāvya* style, shows the way the poet works: *ākalpa-vikalpa-talpa* in line three. The ending, *naiṣā niśāṃ neṣyati*, reproduces Radha's restlessness, impatience, and anguish, carrying the reader back to the opening image of her *bahuśaḥ* (repeatedly) adorning her limbs at the hint of a quavering leaf.

The repeated sounds, repeated ornamentation, repetition of her thoughts—all fit the erotic tension. Elsewhere in the poem, Krishna too has been taken up by furious desire, as he stumbles in and out of the dark *kuñja* (thicket), where he first made love to Radha.

Miller writes, "the redundancies are incessant, complex, and multileveled. They create a sensuous surface of verbal ornamentation that suggests comparison with the sculptured surfaces of the medieval Hindu temples of Bhubaneswar and Khajuraho." Rhythm and repetitive sounds of this sort are used in mantra, liturgy, prayer—all those forms of language which, like poetry, are not meant to describe something, but to propel the speaker or listener into a particular state of mind. Or to provoke supernatural acts. I'm certain that Jayadeva chose the repeated sounds carefully, based on India's archaic science of speech-magic.

परिहर कृतातङ्के शङ्कां त्वया सततं घन-
स्तनजघनयाक्रान्ते स्वान्ते परानवकाशिनि ।
विशति वितनोरन्यो धन्यो न कोऽपि ममान्तरं
स्तनभरपरिरम्भारम्भे विधेहि विधेयताम् ॥
[GG 10.10]

parihara kṛtātaṅke śaṅkāṃ tvayā satataṃ ghana-
stanajaghanayākrānte svānte parānavakāśini
viśati vitanor anyo dhanyo na ko'pi mamāntaraṃ
stanabharaparirambhārambhe vidhehi vidheyatām

parihara. (second-person imp.) give up
kṛtātaṅke. (voc.) (f.) O doubtful one
śaṅkāṃ. uncertainty
tvayā. by you
satataṃ. always
ghana. deep, full, firm
stana. breasts
jaghanaya. loins
ākrānte. when gone
svānte. (loc.) love, in one's own heart
para-anavakāśini. (voc.) O one without a rival, against whom a rival has no chance
viśati. enters
vitanoḥ. bodiless, a spirit or ghost
anyaḥ. other
dhanyaḥ. fortunate
na ko'pi. who is not
mamāntaraṃ. inside me
stana-bhara. breast fullness
parirambha. embrace
ārambhe. when (we) begin
vidhehi. destiny, old custom
vidheyatām. may it be granted

Let the Old Doubts Go

Let the old doubts go,
anguished Radha.
Your unfathomed breasts and
cavernous loins
are all I desire.
What other girl has the power?
Love is a ghost
that has slipped into my entrails.
When I reach to embrace your
deep breasts
may we fulfill the rite
we were born for—

Some of the vocabulary here seems supernatural or spiritual. Radha's body is *ghana* (dark, unfathomable, dense). By contrast the *vitanoḥ* (bodiless spirit or ghost), which is love, has entered Krishna's *antaraṃ* (deep core). The rite, the *vidhehi*, is destiny, fate, old custom, ritual. It is a word that rhymes with the verb that follows, *vidheyatām* (let it be granted). I suspect some kind of coded language—twilight speech or Tantric imagery—in play here. Constantly switching the vocabulary of desire with that of religion or ritual, Jayadeva is also playing the sounds for spiritual-musical effect, beyond the limits of meaning.

In this way, the doubt that the opening words address to Radha is also a religious doubt, directed to the reader, and the power of the poem is to place the reader into Radha's anguished spirit and eroticized organs.

माराङ्के रतिकेलिसंकुलरणारम्भे तया साहस-
प्रायं कान्तजयाय किञ्चिदुपरि प्रारम्भि यत्सम्भ्रमात् ।
निष्पन्दा जघनस्थली शिथिलिता दोर्वल्लिरुत्कम्पितं
वक्षो मीलितमक्षि पौरुषरसः स्त्रीणां कुतः सिध्यति ॥
[GG 12.10]

mārāṅke ratikelisaṃkularaṇārambhe tayā sāhasa-
prāyaṃ kāntajayāya kiñcid upari prārambhi yat sambhramāt
niṣpandā jaghanasthalī śithilitā dorvallir utkampitaṃ
vakṣo mīlitamakṣi pauruṣarasaḥ strīṇāṃ kutaḥ sidhyati

mārāṅke. (loc. abs.) (when) impassioned, inflamed
rati-keli-saṃkula-raṇa-ārambhe. (when) love-play-engaged-pleasure-begun
tayā. by her
sāhasa. recklessly, impulsively, boldly
prāyaṃ. set forth (as in a military campaign)
kānta-jayāya. (with *tayā*) lover-triumphant, conquering her lover
kiñcit. somehow
upari. above, on top
prārambhi. establishing, undertaking (by setting herself)
yat. she, her
sambhramāt. eagerly, excitedly
niṣpandā. (adj.) umoving
jaghana. loins, buttocks, vulva
sthalī. still, stationary
śithilitā. slack, loose (with vines)
doḥ. arms
valliḥ. vine, creeping plant
utkampitaṃ. trembling, heaving (with chest)
vakṣaḥ. chest
mīlitam-akṣi. (bv. cmpd.) closed-eyes
pauruṣa. masculine
rasa. essence, mood, role; savor, delight
strīṇāṃ. (poss.) of women
kutaḥ. how, why
sidhyati. she accomplishes, conquers

Reckless, Inflamed, She Presses Forth

Reckless, inflamed, she presses forth
to the urgent campaign
of sexual love,
flips over and mounts him,
savors the way
he gives in . . .

. . . Later, eyes lidded,
loins cool and no longer rippling,
her arms trail like vines.
Only her chest continues to heave.
Is climbing on top
        what brought her victory?

Through the centuries, Sanskrit poets have portrayed sexual love as a kind of military campaign. Both Vidyā and Vikaṭanitambā wrote poems to warlords—probably patrons—which carry two separate readings. In one reading, the prince's military prowess is glorified; in the second, his success as lover. Other poets have used the trope humorously. From the *Amaruśataka*:

When he's frisky
and steals her undergarments
she squeals in distress
quick—before someone suspects!

But the love god sees,
mighty archer of the Three Worlds

and though the fortifications
are breached,
the erotic struggle decided,
he flashes back to the
battlefield.

[verse 100]

Translated by Andrew Schelling

I think Jayadeva's poem a spiritual event, an enactment. A trace of humor ripples through the stanza, but humor is not his intent. Nor has he composed an allegory of the spirit's relation to the universe's animate energy. He provides a vehicle through which the human spirit can realize that energy.

So what does it mean for the spirit to triumph over the god? Radha achieves victory, which is in fact her own dissolution, through the sexual position known as *viparita* (upside down, or woman on top). What Jayadeva writes is that she took the *puruṣa-rasa* (the masculine role or essence or spirit). Does he mean divine energy lets itself be humbled or conquered? Or is it that masculine and feminine roles get reversed, perhaps absorbed into each other? How does *rati-keli* (the play of love) parallel a military campaign? Radha, after her victory, lies atop her beloved, *jaghana-sthalī* (loins or vulva stilled), as though her spiritual peace is the contrary of Lady Jaghanacapalā's unrequited hunger ("she whose loins are quavering"). Jayadeva leaves with a question: how does *pauruṣa-rasa* among women contribute to mastery? The verb *sidhyati* suggests highest accomplishment, enlightenment; its participle, *siddha*, refers to the most formidable adepts. The metaphysics of Jayadeva's vocabulary insist we enter the question using our own hearts.

Note that the stanza breaks after the second line: the first couplet pictures Radha's energetic lovemaking, the second its aftermath. Hence you feel a huge gap between *saṃbhramāt* (energetically) and *niṣpandā* (motionless). I take the term *rasa* to refer to both her assuming the man's essence (role), and her "savor" in forcing his submission.

श्रीजयदेववचसि रुचिरे हृदयं सदयं कुरु मण्डने ।
हरिचरणस्मरणामृतकृतकलिकलुषभवज्वरखण्डने ।।
[GG 12.19]

śrījayadevavacasi rucire hṛdayaṃ sadayaṃ kuru maṇḍane
haricaraṇasmaraṇāmṛtakṛtakalikaluṣabhavajvarakhaṇḍane

śrī-jayadeva-vacasi. Jayadeva's speech, words
rucire. pleasing
hṛdayaṃ. heart
sadayaṃ. merciful, kind
kuru. (second-person imp.) make, take to heart
maṇḍane. well-crafted
hari. Krishna
caraṇa. feet, wanderings, deeds
smaraṇa. recollection, memory
amṛta. ambrosia, drink of immortality
kṛta. made
kali-kaluṣa-bhava. the Kali Yuga, an evil era
jvara. fever, disease, pestilence
khaṇḍane. dispels, cuts

Reader, Open Your Heart

Reader, open your heart
to Jayadeva's well-
crafted poem. Through it
Krishna's deeds have entered your own memory-stream—
amṛta to cure
Kali Yuga's contagion.

It is hard for me to tell whether Jayadeva means to say Krishna's deeds or his own poem dispels the *jvara* (the fever or infectiousness) of the Kali Yuga. Clearly he means that the drama now resides in our *smaraṇa* (memory). In India's spiritual traditions, *smaraṇa* does not simply mean a cluster of stored detail. It can refer to one's full stream of memory through life—through many lives—or to the recollection of one's essential being, much like Zen's original face. This latter meaning is reinforced by *caraṇa* (deeds or adventures). Literally it is feet, walking, or "way" in the spiritual sense. *Krishna's way is now your own spirit.*

In India's cosmography, the world passes through four *yugas* (epochs), a catastrophic collapse ushering in each successive age, which is more chaotic, degraded, unethical than the previous. Our own, the fourth and final *yuga*—the dark one—is named for Kali or Kālī, Time personified as the death goddess. The Kali Yuga was brought about by the war described in the *Mahābhārata*. Devotion to Krishna seems the final refuge in this age of warfare, social collapse, and natural disaster.

At risk of sounding mundane and technical, here in the Kali Yuga, when ecocide, incessant war, epidemic, and injustice matter so much more, I want to point out that this two-line stanza has an end rhyme: *maṇḍane* and *khaṇḍane*, adjectives that describe Jayadeva's *vacasi* (words or speech or poem). End rhyme is a technique that virtually never showed up in Sanskrit poetry. Jayadeva lifted it from vernacular street song, fit it to his poem, and prefigured the next step in India's art. His eloquent Sanskrit remains impeccable throughout. Objects of affection, longing, or devotion go into the seventh, or locative, case—something like "place your heart in Jayadeva's words."

The second line is a *bahuvṛhi* compound, one long adjective describing the full poem: "made of *amṛta* from recollecting Krishna's feet (and) which dispels the Kali Yuga's pestilence." Again, hard to say if it is Krishna's deeds or Jayadeva's song that is *amṛta* to allay the dark menace.

रचय कुचयोः पत्रं चित्रं कुरुष्व कपोलयोर्
    घटय जघने काञ्चीमञ्च स्रजा कबरीभरम् ।
कलय वलयश्रेणीं पाणौ पदे कुरु नूपुराव्
    इति निगदितः प्रीतः पीताम्बरोऽपि तथाकरोत् ॥
[GG 12.20]

racaya kucayoḥ patraṃ citraṃ kuruṣva kapolayor
    ghaṭaya jaghane kāñcīmañca srajā kabarībharam
kalaya valayaśreṇīṃ pāṇau pade kuru nūpurāv
    iti nigaditaḥ prītaḥ pītāmbaro'pi tathākarot

racaya. (second-person imp.) paint
kucayoḥ. (on my two) breasts
patraṃ. a leaf
citraṃ. color
kuruṣva. (imp.) make, draw
kapolayoḥ. (on my) cheeks
ghaṭaya. place
jaghane. over my loins
kāñcīmañca. underskirt, an ornamental cloth wrapping
srajā. string of flowers
kabarībharam. (in) braided hair
kalaya. arrange
valayaśreṇīṃ. bracelet
pānau. on my hands
pade. on my feet
kuru. place
nūpurau. anklets
iti. thus
nigaditaḥ. told, requested
prītaḥ. her lover (with Krishna)
pītāmbharaḥ. Krishna, "the yellow clothed"
api. (emph.)
tathā. just so
akarot. did

On My Breast Draw a Leaf

"On my breast draw a leaf
paint my cheeks
lay a silk scarf across these dark loins.
Wind into my heavy black braid
white petals,
fit gemstones onto my wrists,
anklets over my feet."
And each thing she desired
her saffron-robed lover
fulfilled.

Back at the start, Jayadeva opened with a stanza that foreshadowed the drama to come. That stanza—ambiguous, hard to fathom, broken with contradictions—has provoked speculation for nine hundred years. After presenting it, he drew back to invoke Vāg-Devī, present his credentials as a poet, compare his work to that of other poets, and note the stories he would draw on for his poem. Now at the close—after taking his reader outside the action with the metaphysical claim of the preceding verse (12.19)—he delivers a final rhyme. The lovers reappear, their passions temporarily spent, recovering self-awareness. Notice the curious inversion. Krishna, the *deva*, is adorning the human woman. He dresses her image as a worshipper would dress the statue of a deity into which the god has descended.

From the *thumri* singer Vidya Rao I heard this: the lovemaking has dissolved Radha; she has been absorbed into her beloved, the energy that animates the cosmos. What now? Who is she? Is she to remain a pulsing raw naked thing? For the play of creation to continue—and the ecstasy of loss and recovery to recur—Radha needs to be restored. Krishna does what she *nigaditaḥ* (requested), reconstructing her identity limb by limb, ornament by ornament. He colors, he wraps, he arranges from her head to her feet. White blossoms of the *tamāla* tree, delicate silver anklets, henna designs on her breasts. Into her braid he winds blossoms; over her loins he lays a silk scarf.

Krishna has become the artist. Maybe Jayadeva thought of himself this way: constructing his poem limb by limb; ornamenting its body verse by verse?

Further Thoughts on the Gīta-Govinda

For people who listen to poetry, the twelth-century Sanskrit *Gīta-Govinda* by Jayadeva is the original love song of Krishna and Radha, his *gopi*, cowherd girl. In it Krishna seems the primal force that animates nature—"like the incarnation [*mūrti*] of erotic love," Jayadeva says.

Those who keep the deeds and songs of Krishna close to their hearts consider him the cosmic power of the Kali Yuga or Dark Age, the last refuge for humans when times grow desperate.

Krishna has many guises—some of which can be traced to India's Paleolithic tribes—all suggesting a telluric or fertility spirit. Anthropologists and scholars cannot locate a single source for his mythology, and the story cycles concerning Krishna are tangled. As the charioteer and friend of Arjuna in the *Bhagavad-Gīta*, he is originator and destroyer of the universe, the source of everything. In the *rati-keli-kathā*, or tales of erotic passion—which Jayadeva acknowledges as his sources for *Gīta-Govinda*—Krishna plays the flute of the nomadic tribesman, and his tunes lure the village women back to the forest. Some see in this a cultural battle between hunting people—or pastoralists who migrate with their herds and do not regard land as property—and those who live by agriculture, setting clear boundaries between cropland and non-arable badlands. The figure of Krishna exposes the fascination and anxiety with which highly regulated agricultural societies regard wilderness and animist lifeways.

In paintings, his color is that of an approaching thunderhead, a shimmering blue-black. In fact his name means black—I'd call the color raven, to distinguish its opalescent blue gleam from matte-black or coal.

Jayadeva was born in Northeastern India: Bengal, Orissa, or Mathura. He excelled at Sanskrit, trained himself as a poet, then took a vow to become a celibate pilgrim. He said he would never stop longer than a single night under the same tree. His wanderings took him to the renowned Jagannatha Temple in the city of Puri, situated on the seacoast in Orissa. In Puri, a brahman attached to the temple had a vision: Jayadeva should marry the brahman's daughter Padmāvatī—a dancer dedicated to the temple—settle in town, and write a poem to Krishna. Jayadeva renounced his vows, married Padmāvatī, and wrote the *Gīta-Govinda.*

Meeting Padmāvatī wakened in Jayadeva the *rasa*, the bedrock emotion, of love. What had been distant accounts of spiritual grace, a theme for poetry, or even a set of metaphysical abstractions, came alive in his own body: the merging of spiritual and erotic ecstasy. Later poets would sing of the *prem-bhakti-marg*, the path of love and devotion, and warn of its razor-sharp edge. But under Padmāvatī's hands, Jayadeva learnt that the old tales, the yogic teachings, were no far-off vision. They were an experience to be tasted through one's senses.

In the fifteenth century, Jayadeva's songs and Padmāvatī's dances were instituted as the official liturgy for the Jagannatha Temple in Puri. I find this weird but inexplicably fitting. Jagannatha, identified with Krishna in ways I do not quite understand, is a starkly tribal deity. His image has barely traveled the road to human form. He seems a black stump of wood with metal platters for eyes, sticks for rudimentary arms, no hands. In India, tribal deities—in fact most localized deities, or *devatā*—are generally not iconic: a post, a heap of stones, a cloth-draped tree. On the beach at Puri in 1993 I saw an entire clan of coconuts, dressed in bright gowns, lined up for worship. Jagannatha's temple, forbidden to non-Hindus, feeds twenty thousand pilgrims a day, "the world's largest kitchen." Jagannatha means "lord of the universe." For six hundred years Jayadeva's *Gīta-Govinda* has been Jagannatha's song.

The *Gīta-Govinda* occurs in twelve cantos. These contain twenty-four songs set to particular *ragas*, or musical modes. Between the songs, Jayadeva has woven narrative verses, which recount the shifting phases of love between Krishna and his "secret" consort, Radha. Their romance is a rite of spring, the dark thickets of the poem fragrant with danger, desire, and uncertainty. In other contexts Krishna performs the *rasamaṇḍala*, his circle dance with numerous consorts, an autumn event bearing residual traces of rutting season. (I find it intriguing to wonder what mammal he emerged from. The Sanskrit word *śṛṅgāra*, erotic love, comes from *śṛṅga*, horn, antler.) Krishna's affair with Radha takes place in early spring, however, when we humans become achingly vulnerable to love and wind, flowers, birdlife, and soft grasses.

Radha's origins are obscure. Her name was first applied to the two-star constellation Viśakha (branched or binary), which was identified with spring and was brightest in the year's first month, Mādhava (moon of honey-gatherers). Mādhava becomes one of Krishna's epithets. The late Barbara Miller, who edited Jayadeva's poem from a study of the various early manuscripts, writes of tracing Radha's name to origins in astronomy and seasonal cycles: "The somewhat esoteric character of these associations may have increased the appeal of Radha as a consort for Krishna in a secret relationship." In its opening verse the *Gīta-Govinda* notes the concealment. The lovers are subject to *rahaḥ-kelaya*, secret desires, which overcome them at night in a thicket along the Yamuna River. Jayadeva's songs follow the lovers, through devastating moods of loneliness and desolation, into rapture.

Sanskrit poets considered love the body's original language and the foremost theme for poetry. You could say that the complex metaphysics of India—heady, magnificent, intricate, contradictory—finally return to a single imperative: love.

I think it the genius of Krishna poetry to take the hair-splitting metaphysics of India, lift them from our easily bewildered minds, and relocate them in the glands and organs of the human body. In the Kali Yuga—so it is believed—not everybody can practice meditation, not everyone wrap the mind around subtle doctrine or follow the eight stages of yoga. Everyone can taste the desolations and ecstasies of love, though. Poetry and song show the way. The Bengali poet Chandidāsa (born around 1408) sang:

> The essence of beauty
> springs from the eternal play
> of man as Krishna
> and woman as Radha.
> Devoted lovers
> in the act of loving,
> seek to reach
> the goal.
>
> *Translated by Deben Bhattacharya*

Jagannatha could be the animating power of nature; Krishna is the eros of human nature, wakened by Radha. Being a constellation, a springtime occurrence, Radha is "a spirit of nature." She dances in our glands. For her, "erotic" and "spiritual" are meaningless distinctions as she approaches her lover. Near the end of Jayadeva's poem, Krishna sings to Radha as *kāminī*, lady of desire. She is pure life force, the spirit that yearns to give love in a dark and cruel era. The same irrepressible longing, Jayadeva's poem says, drives every natural thing. To sing of desire, to name those animated by it—rutting deer, white *tamāla* petals, the brindled moon, the honeybees—reaffirms the oldest biological kinship.

This anyhow is the way I read *Gīta-Govinda.*

I think it worth lingering over the fact that Jayadeva wrote his poem within a century of Dante Alighieri's *Commedia.* Both poets in a sense were bringing to fruition and closing the door on an earlier literature: Jayadeva on classical Sanskrit; Dante on the world of Greek and Roman antiquity. Both poets masterfully worked within the poetic conventions of an earlier time; yet both seem the key innovators for a poetry that would follow. Dante introduced common speech into high poetry, discarding scholastic Latin for the vulgate Italian. Jayadeva wrote his *prabandha,* composition, in classical Sanskrit, but he dignified vernacular tradition by including song forms from folk sources. He also brought into Sanskrit poetry such novelties as end rhyme, which characterizes vernacular song. He included his own name in his poem—not unknown to Sanskrit, but a practice that runs through *bhakti,* devotional poetry, which was emerging in various parts of India in local tongues. And he set the songs of *Gīta-Govinda* to specified *ragas*, the first historical instance known.

Jayadeva regarded himself as an accomplished poet before he composed

Gīta-Govinda. In a couple of opening stanzas, he alerts the reader to his mastery of sound, syntax, meaning, imagery, and *rasa.* Earlier poets, he says, excelled at one or another of these, but he has mastered the range of poetry. To modern ears this sounds boastful. No doubt that's part of it; for his day, though, it demonstrated pedigree and the serious training he'd gone through. I guess you could compare it to American doctors or automobile mechanics displaying certificates of training in their workplaces.

Here then is the culmination of a thousand years or more of classical Sanskrit poetry. It narrates the early love of Krishna and Radha, their separation and anguished estrangement, then their reunion. From Jayadeva's time on, his poem has been received as a vision of the human spirit's relationship to the energy that animates the world.

Bibliography

Amaruśataka. Edited by Narayana Rama Acharya "Kavyatirtha." Mumbai: Nirnaya Sagara Press, 1954.

Amaruśataka. Edited and translated by Chintaman Ramchandra Devadhar. Reprint. New Delhi: Motilal Banarsidass, 1959, 1984.

An Anthology of Sanskrit Court Poetry: Vidyākara's Subhāṣitaratnakoṣa. Translated by Daniel H.H. Ingalls. Cambridge: Harvard University Press, 1965.

Bhartrihari: Poems. Translated by Barbara Stoler Miller. New York: Columbia University Press, 1967.

Chaudhuri, Jatindra Bimal. *Sanskrit Poetesses.* Calcutta: Published by the author, 1941.

Daumal, René. *Rasa, or, Knowledge of the Self: Essays on Indian Aesthetics and Selected Sanskrit Studies.* Translated by Louise Landes Levi. New York: New Directions, 1982.

Kālidāsa. *The Birth of Kumāra.* Translated by David Smith. New York: New York University Press, 2005.

Love Song of the Dark Lord: Jayadeva's Gītagovinda. Translated by Barbara Stoler Miller. New York: Columbia University Press, 1977.

Monier-Williams, Sir M. *Sanskrit-English Dictionary.* Oxford: Clarendon Press, 1899, 1951.

The Paddhati of Śārngadhara. Edited by Peter Peterson. Bombay: Government Central Book Depot, 1888.

Paz, Octavio. *In Light of India.* Translated by Eliot Weinberger. New York: Harcourt Brace, 1997.

The Peacock's Egg. Translated by W. S. Merwin and J. Moussaief Masson. San Francisco: North Point Press, 1981.

A Poem at the Right Moment: Remembered Verses from Premodern South India. Collected and edited by Velcheru Narayana Rao and David Shulman. Berkeley: University of California Press, 1998.